Remembering

Harry Kalas

*The Life of a Phillies Icon
Told by Those Who Knew Him Best*

Rich Wolfe

Printed in U.S.A.
ISBN: 978-1-60078-812-3
Design by The Printed Page
Page production by Patricia Frey
Distributed by Triumph Books LLC

*<u>PAGE TWO.</u> In 1941, the news director at a small radio station in Kalamazoo, Michigan hired Harry Caray who had been employed at a station in Joliet, Illinois. The news director's name was Paul Harvey. Yes, that PAUL HARVEY! "And now, you have the rest of the story . . . .

DEDICATION

To:

Michael Kinsella
of
Newtown Square

(If only I recognized when I first met him
that he needed professional help)

ACKNOWLEDGMENTS

Compiling the material for *Remembering Harry Kalas* was a wonderful experience. There were hundreds of people who cooperated so willingly to make this book special.

The author is personally responsible for all errors, misstatements, inaccuracies, omissions, commissions, fallacies . . . if it's wrong and it's in this book, it's my fault.

Sincere thanks to Ellen Brewer from Edmond, Oklahoma and Lisa Liddy at The Printed Page in Phoenix.

Thanks must also go to Bob Verdi and the *Chicago Tribune*, as well as Leigh Tobin and Larry Shenk of the Philadelphia Phillies . . . also Susan Dianni of the *Inquirer*.

A special tip of the hat to Gordie Jones, Mike Radano, and Kevin Roberts. They were great.

CHAT ROOMS

PREFACE

It was over 50 years ago when I first met Harry Kalas in the Iowa Field House in Iowa City, Iowa. Harry was close to graduation from college. I had just started high school. We were there to watch the much ballyhooed freshman debut of basketball wunderkind Connie Hawkins from Brooklyn, the top recruit in the country that year who, strangely, had opted for Iowa. It ended up that Hawkins was alleged to be in a gambling scandal and never played at Iowa. He didn't play in the NBA for years, but he finally made it with the Phoenix Suns, where his number is retired.

As I'm sitting there, these two young guys, obviously a few years older than I, came in and sat to my right. The guy to my immediate right was Harry Kalas from Le Mars, Iowa. He not only loved basketball and baseball and football, but he was exceptionally knowledgeable about them. The most obvious thing about him, of course, was his voice. He looked very young with his blond hair, but his voice made him sound old. That was it. We talked the whole game, had a great time, and I actually never even knew his name.

Fast-forward a few years, and I'm in the family waiting room at Shea Stadium in 1966. My college roommate had just broken in with the Mets. All of a sudden, I heard "the voice" from behind me! Even though it had been several years, I instantly recognized it. I turned around, re-introduced myself and asked him what he was doing there. I was shocked when he told me he was a play-by-play announcer with the Houston Astros and was there to give a package to Ruth Ryan, Nolan Ryan's wife. Since Ruth wasn't readily available, Harry and I had time for a wonderful talk. We discussed a mutual friend, Paul Maaske, who was the head basketball coach at Cornell College in Mt. Vernon, Iowa, where Harry originally started college. We had a great discussion about why it is that everyone who attends the University of Iowa, no matter where in the country they're from, absolutely loves it.

Many years went by before I talked with Harry again. In 2004, I interviewed him for my *For Hawkeye Fans Only* book. At that time, I sent him a book I had done on Jack Buck—a book that he loved. He asked, "Rich, would you ever consider doing a book like this on me some day?" I said, "Yeah, but let's do it before you pass." He just laughed. At that time, I asked him how much longer he was going to work, and why he was always so nice in signing autographs and making so many public appearances when he had to be tired and wanted to do other things. He said it reminded him of a story he had heard about 10 years before about Dolly Parton. When Dolly Parton was making a movie called *Steel Magnolias*, in the oppressive heat and humidity of Louisiana one summer, all the co-actors were sitting around complaining to high heaven about how bad the conditions were. Finally Sally Field realized that Dolly Parton hadn't said a word— hadn't complained one time. Sally Field said, "Dolly, aren't you hot? Isn't this heat killing you?" Dolly said, "Yes, I'm hot . . . and the heat's killing me, but when I was a little girl, I dreamed of being famous. I dreamed of being a singer. I dreamed of being in the movies. If this is the price I pay for reaching my dream, then it's a pretty cheap price. So, yes, I'm uncomfortable, but it's worth it." Harry said that's how he felt about baseball. He loved baseball so much and wanted to be an announcer so badly from such a young age that no matter how old he got, he would always relish going to the ballpark, meeting fans and talking baseball.

I've been very blessed to do many books, including ones on his fellow announcers Vin Scully, Harry Caray and Jack Buck. Upon completing this Harry Kalas book, it was apparent that there are incredible similarities among those four announcers . . . mainly their manners, their thoughtfulness, their kindness, their work ethic and their incredible attention to detail.

It's amazing the pull baseball announcers have on their fans, probably because fans spend more time listening to the announcers of their favorite team than they do listening to their spouse every summer.

The biggest problem, by far, in doing a Harry Kalas book is every-one—there were no exceptions—went off on long tangents about Harry Kalas' kindness, his generosity, his quick wit, his helpful nature and on and on, with great testimonials about the type of person Harry Kalas was. So, more than 150 pages were deleted from this book because there were constant, similar and dupli-cate testimonials. Even so, many remain.

Since the age of 10, I've been a serious collector of sports books. During that time—for the sake of argument, let's call it 30 years—make it 20—my favorite book style is the eavesdropping type where the subject talks in his own words, without the "then he said" or "the air was so thick you could cut it with a butter knife" waste of verbiage that makes it so hard to get to the meat of the matter . . . Books such as Lawrence Ritter's *Glory of Their Times* and Donald Honig's *Baseball When the Grass was Real,* or any of my friend Peter Golenbock's books like *The Bronx Zoo.*

Thus, I adopted that style when I started compiling oral histories of the Vin Scullys and Harry Carays of the world. I'm a sports fan first and foremost—I don't even pretend to be an author. This book is designed solely for other sports fans. I really don't care what the publisher, editors or critics think. I'm only inter-ested in Phillie fans having an enjoyable read and getting their money's worth. Sometimes a person being interviewed will drift off the subject but if the feeling is that Phillie fans would enjoy their digression, it stays in the book. If you feel there is too much extraneous material, just jot your thoughts down on the back of a $20 bill and send it directly to me. Constructive criticism can be good for one's soul, as well as for the pizza man.

In an effort to get more material into the book, the editor decided to merge some of the paragraphs and omit some of the commas which will allow for the reader to receive an additional 20,000 words, the equivalent of 50 pages. More bang for the buck . . . more fodder for English teachers . . . fewer dead trees.

I'm the least likely person in the country to write a book. I can't type. I've never turned on a computer, and I've never seen the

Internet. I refuse to sit in press boxes and corporate suites. I have a belief that the cheaper the seat, the better the fan. No matter where you sit, you have to sit back and admire Harry Kalas as you reflect on his incredible career. He's the definition of a true professional, and we could all learn from his humility.

I only write books on people who seem admirable from a distance. The fear, once you start a project, is the subject will turn out to be a jerk. With Harry Kalas' intensity and quest for perfection it could easily follow that he could have been a self-absorbed, arrogant, rude boor like many people in his business. As you will soon find out, you would want your son, your brother, your husband or your friends to possess these qualities of humbleness, thoughtfulness, joy for living, a passion for his job and the love of baseball that Harry Kalas had. If you are a certain age in this country, there are maybe three or four people in your lifetime that you remember where you were when you heard they had died—John F. Kennedy, Elvis, Princess Diana and, since you are reading this book, probably Harry Kalas.

It's unusual to talk about Harry Kalas in the past tense because repeatedly during interviews most of his friends and cohorts would talk about him in the present tense.

When you find out more about Harry Kalas and how he achieved his success while keeping his values, you have to ask the question, "Why can't everybody be as nice as Harry Kalas?" There is nothing he did that was very difficult. He was very kind. He was hard working. He had all these values that everyone could possess if they wanted.

It's also interesting—as you'll find in this book—how some people will view the same happening in completely different terms. There was a thought of omitting the attempts at humorous headlines—some of the headlines in this book prove that truly great comedy is not funny—since the book was written after Harry's death. But, all of Harry's friends who were questioned in this matter unanimously nixed that idea.

At the bottom of certain pages you will see factoids that relate to a topic stated in the text. That's where I pretend that Harry Kalas is leaning down to do the color commentary for his book.

Harry Kalas was an unorthodox man in a society where orthodox behavior has stifled creativity, adventure and fun . . . a society where posturing and positioning one's image in order to maximize income has replaced honesty and bluntness . . . a difference-maker on an indifferent planet . . . a man the way men used to be in an America that is not the way it used to be . . . a loyal man to colleagues, classmates and friends in an age when most people's loyalties are in the wallet . . . a man who fought the good fight and lived the good life.

We'll never forget Harry Kalas because memories of people like Harry Kalas never grow old.

—Rich Wolfe
   Behind a messy desk in sunny Cape Cod

PROLOGUE

Harry Kalas
Todd Kalas
Eileen Kalas
David Montgomery

IOWA? IT'S ON ALL THE MAPS NOW

[The following is an excerpt from the author's 2004 book
For Hawkeye Fans Only]

Harry Kalas

Former WSUI sportscaster Harry Kalas was enshrined in Baseball's Hall of Fame in Cooperstown in 2002. He has been "God" for 33 years as the Voice of the Philadelphia Phillies. He also replaced the legendary John Facenda for NFL Films. Urban myth held that Kalas worked at a gas station in Mt. Vernon, Iowa, while going to Cornell College . . . and a regular customer—in those days of full service only—said, "With that voice, you have to become a broadcaster" . . . whereupon Kalas transferred to The University of Iowa and majored in communications. "Not so!" says Kalas.

I graduated from Naperville High School in west suburban Chicago fifty years ago. My dad was a minister so just by virtue of being a "**P.K.**"*—preacher's kid, I got a partial scholarship to Cornell College in Mt. Vernon, Iowa. I was there for one year and got into a little trouble. They asked me not to come back. Cornell was a church-affiliated school, and unfortunately, in those years, I was inclined to have a beer or two. I got great encouragement while at Cornell from a blind speech professor, Walter Stroemer. I knew that I wanted to be a sportscaster, even in high school, and he really encouraged me to do it.

I was working at radio station, KPIG, in Cedar Rapids during the summer. Those were the actual call letters of the station. I

***P. K.** Wrigley and Milton Hershey were bitter business rivals. When Wrigley bought the Chicago Cubs, Hershey tried to buy the Philadelphia Phillies . . . and sell chocolate gum. Hershey failed in both efforts.

wanted to continue my college education and it was suggested that I go to Iowa University because they had a good communications school. That's how I ended up there.

Going to Iowa City was one of the best moves I ever made. I pledged Phi Delta Theta, and Randy Duncan was also a member. I got involved at the campus station, WSUI, and got great experience there doing all the Hawkeye sports. Every sports event the Hawkeyes were involved in, we were out there with microphones making fools of ourselves. But, what great experience! Randy Duncan was a big guy there. Being in the same fraternity, he really helped me a lot as far as Hawkeye football players and the teams they were playing. I did baseball and basketball games for the campus station. You didn't have all the information about the players you would like to have, so it was just feeling your way through the game and trying to call the game.

I just got in the mail that they're having an Airliner reunion. I worked at the Airliner when I was in school, washing pots and pans. It was good because after I finished my work, I was one of those "at the bar." It was the hot spot on campus.

THE SON ALSO RISES

Todd Kalas

Todd Kalas, Harry's oldest son, followed his father into the broadcast booth and is the play-by-play announcer for the Tampa Bay Rays—which provided a wonderful conflu- ence of events in 2008, when the Rays and the Phillies played in the World Series. The respec- tive local television stations arranged for them to do some innings together. Before becoming the Rays' broadcaster in 1998, Todd worked as a broadcaster with the Phillies from 1994– 96 in an official capacity—after working in the booth for years in an unofficial capacity when he was growing up.

It was always part of the fabric of growing up—that Dad was on TV, so it didn't really faze us too much. You knew that he did something different based on the reaction of some of the kids in elementary school; they'd ask us whether our dad knew Mike Schmidt, or Greg Luzinski, or Larry Bowa. But other than that, it was just always there. Dad was always on TV or on the radio. That was just part of it.

I was the instigator of getting Dad to the Phillies party at the Hall of Fame. He was so wrapped up in whatever the protocol was— he had to be here for a certain amount of time and then he had to be there for a certain amount of time. They had a schedule for him pretty tight for the whole weekend at Cooperstown. But we knew the Phillies were having their own party, and I kept saying, "Dad, we should try to get over there." He said he didn't know if he could leave this or that dinner, so I talked to the Hall of Fame people and they said, "Absolutely, by all means, go and be a part of that." So we scooted over there for 15 or 20 minutes, just enough time for him to hang out and see everybody and sing "High Hopes." That was probably, for me, the most special part of the weekend. For him, deep down, the induction ceremony itself was huge. But being a part of that Phillies celebration was really special for him.

It was crazy, because it was the first time I'd ever been to Cooperstown. First time. I would have liked to have gone when Mike Schmidt was inducted, but the whole other broadcast team went that year—so I was actually filling in for the guys who went to go see Schmidty get inducted on the Phillies telecast. So that was my first trip to Cooperstown, and to go there with your dad going into the Hall of Fame . . . that was the pinnacle of everything. It was so incredible to be a part of that weekend. The little, small moments throughout that weekend were great.

Just sitting out on the lake there, reminiscing, being part of this incredible moment, the highest honor for a broadcaster—and that was something my dad wanted to do his whole life—it was hard to ever top something like that. Just being around the whole scene. Like when I first checked into the hotel—I'm coming into my room, and right across the hall Stan Musial is opening his door. Staying in the same hotel with Stan Musial is one thing, but that he's just across the hall, to be his neighbor for a few days, was just crazy. . . .

Becoming a baseball broadcaster myself, it happened probably more subconsciously early because I was always around it. Everybody thought I would eventually end up in the broadcast booth because I kept my own scorebook for every game I ever went to when I was little. I would keep my own stats for just the games I saw, and when I was probably 12 or 13 I was in the broadcast booth helping out with the out-of-town scoreboard on Sunday afternoon. So everybody thought that was going to be a natural progression—that I would end up in the broadcast booth. But at some point, I wanted to do my own thing. I tried to find my own niche. I went to the University of Maryland and tried a bunch of different majors—always thinking in the back of my mind that at some point I might try broadcasting. It was like I wanted to see if there was something out there I could fall in love with, but I finally just decided to go to Syracuse to see if I was made to be a broadcaster, whether I had the talent for it. It was there when I decided I might try to make a run at it.

There's no doubt, this is a great job to be able to call games, to go to the ballpark for a living. I love the travel, I love sports. That's all great. But it was always how much Dad enjoyed it. Watching that as a kid, that definitely rubs off on you. There's no way that can't leave an indelible impression. Because he did. He loved every single minute of what he did. He couldn't wait to get to the ballpark. He stayed busy in the offseasons, too. But baseball was his pulse. He was always around the stadium, loved being around the team, loved being around the fans. There wasn't one, small, tiny aspect of it—even the travel, he didn't seem to mind—there wasn't one aspect of what he did that he didn't love.

I'm not sure where "High Hopes" came from. I was probably about 12 when I heard him sing it for the first time. He sang it at one of his birthdays. It was weird because it wasn't like a lot of people joined in. He just sang it. It was like, "OK, Harry must be having a good time, he's singing." But I thought, "Well, that's probably the last time he does that." But lo and behold, he came out again the 39th birthday and sang it. And again at his 40th birthday. It just became his go-to song. I don't know why he loved it so much. But it was his favorite song to sing.

During the '93 season, that's when it became the thing to do after big Phillies wins. That was special, because it really was just a little song that he used to do at his birthday celebrations or occasionally at a piano bar—and then it became his theme song with the Phillies. . . .

We worked the first inning of the first game of the 2008 World Series together, at Tropicana Field, on the Phillies radio network. It was so much fun. The Phillies had already gotten into the World Series. So when the Rays were playing Game Seven of the ALCS against the Red Sox, that was probably the most intense I've ever been watching a game because I knew the opportunity that was at hand. I was so excited when the Rays were able to win the ALCS, knowing that we were going to be at the World Series together.

It was Dad's idea; he went to Rob Brooks, the Phillies' director of broadcasting, and asked if we could do an inning together. And Brooksy made it happen. That inning was cool, but mostly it was just being around each other and spending that whole week together. That was amazing. Just for the Rays to even think about the World Series was a real long shot, and to be able to play the Phillies was even more unlikely. The whole thing just played out perfectly. I totally was in the moment at all times, and I cherish every second we had.

We always had a good time. A lot of Wiffle Ball games, and football in the fall. He always made time for us. He was gone a lot, but that was part and parcel of what he did for a living. We understood that growing up. To me, the best times of the year were always in March. Up until high school, we got out for the whole month, went down to spring training, got tutors, and we spent the whole month together. We'd do beach stuff, miniature golf, spring training games. We basically had a whole month where Dad was working days and then he was home every night. So that was really cool. That, to me, was the best time of the year.

He was always there. He was always around. He made sure he spent a lot of time with us when he was home. We knew he had a busy schedule, but we had a lot of fun.

We spent a lot of time at the stadium, too, in the summer, and that was nice. We'd get to the ballpark at 3:30 or 4 o'clock. That was back in the days of the press room, too, so we sometimes didn't get home until late. When Pete Rose was here, we used to hang out with his kids, and Garry Maddox's kids were a little younger than us, but they'd be there. We had all kinds of games; we'd run the bases; there was a basketball court down in the tunnel; we could go in the batting cages. It was like our own personal playground.

Dad got a sense of how people felt about him in 2002, at the Hall of Fame induction. I think that surprised him, the number of tributes, the outpouring. He was almost embarrassed, that weekend in Cooperstown. He was that humble, that lacking in ego, that it was almost embarrassing that there would be that much attention paid to him. He had a bit of a sense of how much he meant to the area, but it was never comfortable for him to recognize that because he always just thought of himself as HK—no better than the guy next door, a man devoid of ego, really. He was never quite comfortable really recognizing the impact he had on people.

I don't think he ever could have imagined what happened after he passed. It would have overwhelmed him to know that there was that much love out there for him.

I knew it. I knew there was a special deal going on with Dad and the fans. Every tribute, everything the Phillies or anybody ever did for him, it was always a huge outpouring of love from the fans. But I was aware of it to an extent. But I don't know if I would have known how big that whole week that followed was, or how big the ceremony at the ballpark was. It was incredible. I don't know if I knew the enormity of the affection that the fans held for him.

The whole week it was strong, the support and the emotion we saw from people, but that day was one of the most amazing tributes I've ever seen.

POETRY IN NOTION

Eileen Kalas

Eileen and Harry Kalas were married for 20 years. A very private person, Eileen Kalas rarely gives interviews and attended Phillies games only sparingly—although she was always with her husband when Harry was being honored, or when their son Kane was singing the National Anthem. Richie Ashburn, knowing Eileen eschewed attention and disliked the spotlight, would playfully ask her to stand to be recognized at banquets—and then pretend not to see her, forcing Eileen to keep standing for several minutes. In poems written about Eileen, Harry described her as "Strong as the pounding surf/yet gentle as Bluegrass turf."

Given Harry's love for poetry, Eileen Kalas asked that some family poems be included in this project—one written by Harry for children with cancer, whom he visited in a local hospital, and one written by four-year-old Kane for his father on Father's Day.

"The Journey"
Harry Kalas

Now it seems like a tunnel of dark
There is no light, there is no spark

But wait, did I see light?
Can I let go of my wonder and fright?

Yes, I can see sunshine and a rainbow
I can see stars in the sky and I know

The angels around me are real
But ask me tomorrow and I'll tell you how I feel.

"The Greatest Dad in the World"
Kane Kalas,

I've got a dad, he's very kind
but sometimes he's hard to find

He's always going to and fro
from Philadelphia to San Diego

He does Phillies games day and night
he's so nice it's kind of a fright

When he gets home he's not that neat
but Mom still thinks he's really sweet

As for me I think he's great
Isn't this some wonderful fate!

MEET THE PREZ

David Montgomery

David Montgomery is the Phillies' president and chief executive officer, and as general partner he is the public face of the team's ownership group. He grew up a Phillies fan, watching games at Connie Mack Stadium. He continued his love affair with baseball and the Phillies as a college student at Penn—where he befriended future Philadelphia mayor and Pennsylvania governor Ed Rendell. After Harry Kalas passed away before a Phillies game in Washington, it was Montgomery who made the announcement, uttering the perfect, poignant sentence: "We've lost our voice."

Harry and I started with the Phillies the same year—1971. My memory of his work started the night we opened the Vet in 1971: We played the Expos that day. The Saturday before, April 3, we had a dedication ceremony. Now, I grew up with By Saam and Bill Campbell, and I probably was in that category of people who were curious to see how Kalas would do. And there he is, in a trenchcoat, with all this blond hair. And right away, you saw his style. He was so at ease behind the microphone. I just remember thinking, "This guy's got it."

Those early years, it was such a dream to be working in baseball, and for me the press club postgame in those days was a really special experience for a young person. That was where I learned a lot of the nuances of the game. In addition to the broadcast people, the scouts were always there, the media, the people who worked for the club. And there was this larger-than-life, center-of-the-party type of person in the middle of it—that was Harry. He loved that dialogue, loved pulling people in. I was young enough then that I could stay there very late. But those conversations, the dissecting of the game, went on there every night. People enjoyed hanging out there, and I was just like a sponge—wow, I was working with Richie Ashburn and talking baseball with all these people.

I started with the Phillies as a ticket representative, you'd call it at that time. I would sell season tickets, and I worked with Richie Ashburn a lot. Richie helped sell tickets in those days and got a commission. He was always telling me how close he was to com-mission—and it was my job to complete the sale. And you can imagine Richie saying, "This is the hottest group of leads you'll ever see, boys. Watch your hands—they're red hot! My whole livelihood is in your hands, boys."

Harry loved to talk baseball and learn about the game, and that was the opportunity to do it. That's why a lot of their conversa-tions on the air came out the way they did—Harry was "leading" the witness. He knew what Whitey thought; whether he wanted to bunt in certain situations. That was part of their great byplay.

One of the things that helped Harry in those early days was that he got the biggest endorsement you could get—Richie. Every-body figured out right away, hey, Richie really likes this guy. And if it was good enough for Ashburn, it was good enough for any-body. On top of that, he was smooth, he had the voice, he was really good. And Harry, of course, to the day he died, would ref-erence that—he never did a public performance without talking about how his Whiteness was up there watching. They clicked.

Just as they had all those lines in the booth, that's the way they were out of the booth, too. It wasn't an act; that's how they were. On the golf course, Whitey could not putt well—and Harry was very good. Whitey had all this false bravado: "Boys, this is the perfect distance for me." Invariably when it got down to an impor-tant putt, Harry would say: "Whitey, tell me about this putt." And Whitey would go on and on . . . and when he'd miss it, he'd go, "Phooey!"—never any vulgarity, just *phooey*—and toss the club. And then we'd get in the cart to go on to the next hole and Whitey would say: "Do you know you're riding with a two-time National

League batting champion?" Whitey was such an extraordinary athlete, but golf was the one game that humanized him. Harry loved to tee it up and say, "Whitey, what do you think about this shot?" They'd go back and forth the same way whether they were in the booth or not.

We always had Harry come to our sponsor's golf outing. We had a putting contest around Harry because he was the self-proclaimed "World's Greatest Putter." We'd have different people compete for the right to go against the king, the world's greatest putter. Harry was amazing. To this day I don't know how he performed so well in that. When the ball was going in, Harry loved to say: "Ker-plunka!" And the ball would fall into the cup, and he would stand there proudly with his putter. That was Harry. Whether it was at piano bars or on the putting green, he was at the center of things, the hub, getting others to enjoy themselves. That's what pulled so many of us toward him.

Harry never missed an ALS luncheon. Not only did he do the ALS auction down here, he was so generous with his time with the community. It was because he liked people. That senior citizens place where he would go sing carols every year, it always came at a busy time for us, so we couldn't always support it. But he'd be in here recruiting half dozen of our staff people to go with him. Harry made time for everybody.

I parked next to Harry and Ashburn at the Vet. I got to witness firsthand how generous he was, and how gracious he was to our fans. Richie had his own style, and he was very good, but he'd keep moving—give you the sense that he had somewhere to go. *Hey, how you doing, sure, happy to*—but keep moving. Harry would stand by his car, having these conversations. There were people he had a strictly 81-game relationship with—the same people, night after night. They'd wait for him for two hours, and when he got out there he'd be in no hurry.

I always like to say with our current club, we're very lucky in that the fan support is twofold. The fans like our team as players, and they like them as people. Well, that's how it was with Harry. They liked him as an announcer. They loved him as a person.

Harry's position was always that he could do the whole thing. He wanted to do every game. We would be more likely to say as he went from one season to another that Harry could do whatever he wanted. We'd say to him, "You don't have to do every one." But his position was that if there was a game, he was doing it. I remember talking to him once when he really wasn't feeling well, but he promised he'd be in the next day. I said that really wasn't necessary. He said, "But it's a TV game!" And I said, "It's just an exhibition!" He just believed that this is where he belonged.

I can honestly tell you there was no way we were ever going to say to Harry, "OK, there's the door." Never. Ever. We would have taken him in a reduced role, whatever he wanted. But he felt that it was a long season, he was part of it, he was going to be there. You know what was really important to him? To hang on to his time on the radio. He loved that medium. He loved to be able to paint the picture.

When I think of Harry, I think of how he placed the fans in front of himself. He always encouraged the players to get out there more, sign some autographs, participate. Harry enjoyed it so much. He was so much fun, so much fun to be around. I don't mean to reference **REGGIE JACKSON*** here, but Harry was the straw that stirred the drink for people.

People loved him because they knew how much he loved people. That extra spark, that sparkle that he provided to us all, just pulled us all toward him.

The factoids at the bottom of certain pages just might be "Harry's Color Commentary". Just Might Be.

*In **REGGIE JACKSON**'s last ten October games, he was 7 for 44 with one home run and 14 strikeouts. . . . Only 3 of Mr. October's 18 October home runs put his team in the lead.

Chapter One

HEAR ME NOW, LISTEN TO ME LATER

Larry Andersen
Chris Wheeler
Scott Graham
Andy Musser
Tim McCarver
Curt Smith
Ray Tipton

The Broadcasters

IT'S HARD TO CHEER
WITH A BROKEN HEART

Larry Andersen

Larry Andersen pitched in the majors for 17 years for six teams—including two tours with the Phillies. Known as one of the true characters of the game, Andersen pitched for the 1983 and 1993 World Series teams armed with one of the game's best sliders. He was a pitching coach in the Phillies' minor league system when Richie Ashburn passed away, and was the natural choice to join the broadcast crew. Now in his 12th season in the booth with the Phillies, Andersen and partner Scott Franzke have won Philadelphia Achievement in Radio Awards for Best Live Sports Event Coverage. Andersen's nickname was "L. A."—which Harry Kalas often expanded to "L. A. Breakdown" and then simply "Breakdown." At Kalas' memorial service at Citizens Bank Park, Andersen did a courtly bow to Kalas' casket—a subtle and touching salute to a dear friend.

When I moved into the booth, he basically said, "Whatever you want to do, just go do it. When you've got something to say, you just say it and I'll get out of your way." But, especially the first year, instead of doing what I was supposed to be doing, I just sat there and listened to him. I just loved to listen to him call a game. He made it really easy; he didn't critique me or do anything except say, "Be yourself."

You know how people say Harry never said a bad word about anybody? Well, that was true. He never did. But if I made a mistake on the air? I could say something he wouldn't respond to, but if I made a mistake he was on it. In a heartbeat. He loved it, and it was fun because it was part of what Harry was. He didn't bury you. Just in a very fun way, he'd subtly throw you right under the bus.

One time I was talking about Doug Eddings, an umpire, and as an inside joke I called him "Stadium" Eddings. And Harry said, "Yeah. His friends call him Doug." Once when Kevin Brown was pitching, and I mistakenly said he was the next hitter, Harry said, "Well, that's going to be tough for **KEVIN BROWN***, because he's pitching, too." He had such great timing. He just did it in a funny way, and I was thrilled. He was just acting the same way he did when it was he and Whitey in the booth. Every time he'd throw a little jab at me, I was thrilled. It was so much fun.

There was a game the Phillies won on a balk. Harry said, "Oh, you don't want to win that way." I'm saying that of course you do—you want to win any way you can. Harry starts arguing that it shouldn't have been a balk because the pitcher didn't deceive the runner, and I said, "It's a balk! A balk is a balk is a balk!" And, yeah, I heard about that for a while: "A balk is a balk is a balk, L.A."

That was where Harry was funniest—his timing. We'd be on a plane stranded on the runway, I mean sometimes we'd sit on the runway for three hours without moving, and after an hour or so Harry would turn to you and say, "Pretty smooth flight so far, huh, pal?"

We were in New York once and Harry is singing in a piano bar, and a guy comes through the front door—and he's completely naked, covered in who-knows-what, he's really messed himself up. And he bursts through the door, spins around and collapses right there in front of everybody. Right down. Everybody just gasps, the place is completely silent, and Harry says, "Was my rendition of 'High Hopes' that bad? Was I off-key?"

*The first $100 million contract was given to **KEVIN BROWN** by the Dodgers in 1998. Ten years later 15 players had $100 million contracts.

Harry loved to smoke. And there's no smoking in Citizens Bank Park except for one very select area that we now call the HK Lounge. He used to say, "Pal, I love smoking so much that if I could find someone to hold 'em for me I'd smoke in my sleep."

In 1993, when we clinched, Harry had this paisley tie. He got drenched with champagne, and I wound up with his tie. In fact, I still have it. I found it just the other day when I was going through some stuff. I wore it in the postseason, every game—my tie plus his tie. It was dried out, it was stiff, it still had the champagne stench on it. It's still a little stiff. And after the World Series, there's a picture of us coming off the plane and I'm right behind Harry. I've got both ties on. I'm holding up two fingers; people thought I was giving the peace sign but in reality I was, sadly, saying: "We're number two." Harry got that picture, and he gave it to me, and he signed it: "To L. A.—You're number one in my book."

> I'm not real sure who picked the ties, but they are classic Harry ties.

For Harry's services, Todd and Harry's wife Eileen and the family came in and gave me three of Harry's ties that I could wear for the services. Todd said, "We brought you the three worst ties we could find." I said, "You did a pretty good job." Somebody was talking about this polka-dotted tie Harry had, but Todd said, "Oh, no; that's one of the good ones." I'm not real sure who picked the ties, but they are classic Harry ties. I still have them; four Harry ties—the one from '93 and three of Harry's worst ties. And they'll be worn.

Nobody else could pull off the clothes Harry wore. He had those white shoes, as everyone knows. This is true—one time he needed a new pair of white shoes, and he could not find a pair he liked. Just couldn't find a decent pair of white shoes. So he bought a pair of black shoes and had them dyed white.

Todd Kalas was talking about how after Harry first passed, it was unbelievable—the support and everything the fans said. Todd said, "I can't believe how beloved he was in this city." Harry never acted like it. But he had a sense of that; you'd have to think he did. Maybe Harry didn't realize it to a certain extent. I think he had an idea. I hope so.

My memory of Harry is always going to be when we clinched in '93, with him singing "High Hopes" in the trainer's room and all the guys gathered around. We're all back in the trainer's room, where nobody but players could ever go—no media, no front office, nobody. Except Harry. He was like a freshman who'd pledged but didn't have to go through initiation. He was one of us. When he was hanging out with the players, in the clubhouse or in the back of the plane, or wherever, that was his fixture.

After Harry died, I was interviewed and I said something like, "I don't know if I ever want to hear that song again." I don't think people understood what I meant. I don't want to hear anyone else sing "High Hopes." I don't want to see anyone else try to pick it up and make it their tradition. That's Harry's song. But to listen to Harry sing it? They could play that tape of him singing that song at the ballpark every day. I could listen to Harry sing "High Hopes" anytime.

COLUMBUS DIDN'T STOP AND ASK DIRECTIONS . . . WHY SHOULD HARRY?

Chris Wheeler

Chris Wheeler began his Phillies career as assistant director of publicity and public relations under Larry Shenk in 1971— the same year that David Montgomery joined the team in the ticket office and Harry Kalas arrived to become the Voice of the Phillies. A graduate of Penn State University, "Wheels" now enters his 33rd year as a Phillies broadcaster, doing play-by-play and color analysis on both radio and television.

Here's the Harry story I like to tell:

You know the old joke about how men are bad with directions, but they won't stop and ask? Well, Harry was the worst with directions. He could never find anyplace. I used to have this big Christmas party at my house. Everybody used to come, the players, front office people. This happened more than once—Harry got lost on the way to my house. He'd been to my house I don't know how many times, but he'd get lost.

Harry stopped some strangers on the street, just some kids. He said, "Boys, do you know how to get to Chris Wheeler's house?" He knew the address, he just couldn't find it. They tried to give him directions, but finally Harry just asked them to take him there—they'd drive, and he'd follow. He told them there was a party, and if they'd get him there, they could come with him.

So here comes Harry, bopping into my house, with these complete strangers in tow. There's Greg Luzinski there, Garry Maddox, all these Phillies players, and these kids were just in heaven. They thought it was great. But some of the people there were making "hide the silverware" jokes. They didn't know what to make of it.

Harry was notorious for that; he did it once at a friend's house, a really nice place where they were having an engagement party. He comes in with these complete strangers who'd helped him find the place. And he asks me, "Is this OK?" I'd say, "No, of course it's not!"

But that was Harry. He just collected people. It was like he wanted everybody he met to join the party.

> ... here comes Harry, bopping into my house, with these complete strangers in tow.

It's fair to say that the fans took a while to warm up to Harry. I was a fan then, when he arrived. I got hired in May of that year, and I had to wait until after I did my **ARMY RESERVE*** duty, so I started in July. Bill Campbell was really popular and nobody knew who Harry was. But it wasn't like it would be now. There was no talk radio, there wasn't all the different media that would have stirred it up. There was something there, there was an undercurrent, but it wasn't a big deal because there wasn't all the nonsense you might have seen today.

Harry never complained, never said anything bad about anybody, never complained about anything. Even in 1980, when he couldn't do the World Series, it bothered him—but did he spend a lot of time going over to people and talk about how unfair it was? No. That was the way it was, that was the network agreement, the way it had always been.

---

*Nolan Ryan is the last Major League baseball player to lose playing time during a season due to **MILITARY SERVICE**. When Ryan was with the Mets, he served in the National Guard.

CHOICE VOICE

Scott Graham

A University Pennsylvania graduate, Graham always wanted to became a Phillies broadcaster and in 1992 he joined the Phillies first as a pre-game host and eventually the play-by-play man. Over the course of that time he became very close with Harry Kalas to the extent that he spoke at Kalas grave site on the day he was buried.

The two things that really stand out, the two jokes he stuck with the longest are also my favorites and always made me laugh.

The first one began in 1993 at the World Series in Toronto before Game 1. It was my third year and I was still doing the pregame show. We were doing a pre-pre-game show, about two hours before the game was going to start and I was in the booth with Harry and a production assistant.

We had a system worked out that the operations manager for 1210 WCAU radio, John Weber, would get guests down in the dugout where we had a headset set up. When John would get a guest, he come out of the dugout and wave his arms and the assistant with me would put his headset on and get the name and then pass it to me. The whole time I was on the air, going through what to expect from the game and then, whenever we had an interview, I cut to that person.

For example, if we got Dave Hollins, I'd say something like "Now joining us, from the dugout, Phillies third baseman Dave Hollins." And it worked well for the whole show with one exception.

Everything was going to plan, John waved his arms, the assistant put his headphones on and passed me a piece of paper. The paper read "Duke Raggola." Now, this was before the Internet so it wasn't like I could check to see who this was in a timely manner. I really had no idea who this was and I thought I was pretty well versed on former players or executives or coaches. I really thought I knew baseball and this Duke Raggola was someone I had never heard of.

Anyway, I look back down on the field and John was waving his hands again, only with more energy. He was waving frantically so my assistant, who honestly was not a baseball fan and didn't know the history, put his headphones on, and shook his head that it was "Duke Raggola."

So I tried to bluff my way though it. I said, "And now were pleased to be joined here before Game 1 of the World Series by Duke Raggola. Duke, thanks for joining us, what brings you here." Then I hear the voice on the other side of the line say, "Uh, Scott, this is Joe Garagiola."

That's right, Joe Garagiola. I knew **JOE GARAGIOLA***.

Now, I recovered and we made it through the interview but as I already pointed out, Harry is in the booth and he hears the entire exchange. Until the day Harry died, every chance he got, he asked me about my old friend "Duke Raggola."

We were in Arizona once and I was in the radio booth and Harry was down the hall in the television booth. During the game, he came down to the radio booth, tapped me on the shoulder and said, "Did you see who was down there tonight Scott? It's that Duke Raggola."

I remember being in the office at Citizens Bank Park and Harry had just left the room. He got to the elevator, looked at the television and came back to the office. He called me out to look at the

---

*When **JOE GARAGIOLA** played for the Cardinals, his wife Audrey was the organist at Sportsman's Park, the home of the Cardinals. In 1990 all but two stadiums had an organ, now less than half of the parks have one.

television and pointed out "Look Scott, it's that Duke Raggola."

He just never let anything go and you know what, every time it was funny.

After I got fired in 2006, a year later in the off-season I called my house and my wife answered. I asked if we had any mail and she said I had received a package. I told her to open it and she said it was an early copy of the **BOOK*** *Just Play Ball*, by Joe Garagiola. I said, "Wait a second, check the inside cover."

My wife then read the inscription "Dear Scott, thought you might enjoy an advance copy of my new book, 'Just Play Ball,' Duke." It was written in that Harry scrawl.

> . . . to put that kind of effort into the joke was, first of all, pure Harry.

I can't begin to explain how important that was to me. It's not as if he was sitting next to me and handed it to me. He took the time to autograph it, find my address, and then mail it to my home. To me, to put that kind of effort into the joke was, first of all, pure Harry. But more importantly to me, it was important and just a great feeling that he felt compelled to send it to me even though I hadn't seen him in a while.

Harry believed that we were the owners of what happened on the field each game. If you did the third inning, what happened that inning was on you. It was a time-honored tradition in radio that this was our responsibility.

So, if he did the first three innings of a game and the Phillies scored five runs, he took responsibility. If I followed in the fourth, and the Phillies gave up six runs, he'd come on from the booth, from wherever he was, look down on you, shake his head and then just wave you off.

---

*The Red Sox hold the record for most **BOOKS** written about one team followed by the Yankees and the Brooklyn Dodgers.

He'd look on you with disdain and every time, I laughed. This was not just for me, but for every broadcaster he ever worked with. Just ask Tom McCarthy. His first year, Harry swore that he always had more runs scored so we kept score and Tom was in on it. Harry was convinced he would win but the scary thing was Tom was awful. He had the worst year possible. Every night it seemed like he had the worst inning and without fail, Harry would come in, look at him in disdain and then wave him off.

> It's the last thing Harry ever said to me and I don't think I'd have it any other way.

With our schedule, Harry always had the fourth inning off. Anyway, he'd go back into the office and watch the game or go out in the stairway and smoke a cigarette. Meanwhile, we'd be doing the game and whenever something went wrong, we'd cringe and wait for it, and sure enough, Harry would come in and wave us off.

Now, I hadn't been to Citizens Bank Park since I was fired in 2006, but I was there on opening day for the XM pregame show. After I did my show, I went to the press cafeteria and had dinner with Buck Martinez and Chip Carey. Harry stops by and talks with all of us and then leaves.

I'm still sitting there when Atlanta's Brian McCann hits a home run in the fourth inning that gives the Braves the lead. A minute later, I feel a slap on my shoulder and it's Harry.

"You know what I have to go do now?" Harry said.

It had been two years and I really had forgotten what he was doing.

"I've got to go wave off Phillies radio play-by-play man Scott Franzke." I watched Harry walk down the hall, enter the radio booth, I heard the laughter and smiled.

It's the last thing Harry ever said to me and I don't think I'd have it any other way.

HARRY KALAS MEMORIES ARE FREE AND THEY'RE WORTH EVERY PENNY

Andy Musser

Andy Musser, 71, joined Harry on the Phillies' broadcast team for 26 years, ending in 2001. He now serves as the East Coast representative for the San Francisco–based Anchor Brewing Company.

Harry was the most gentlemanly of men. He was unbelievable to work with. He was already there when I was hired, but he would often ask my opinion of something. We were supposed to wear jackets on the air, and Rich Ashburn and I would ask, "OK, which jackets do you want to wear? It's up to you; you're the lead guy." He'd say, "Oh no, you guys decide." Working around him, you realized the esteem he was building up in the community.

It was a little intimidating to join the broadcast team in 1976. I had been as a youth a fan of the great By Saam. I wrote him some letters, and he was kind enough to answer them. In a sense I didn't replace By Saam. Harry became the No. 1 guy in the booth.

Usually every person listening to the radio becomes a fan of the person they're listening to. It's almost inevitable. I didn't have any particular reason for becoming a fan of Saam's, except he was the announcer for the As and Phillies, and I was listening to him.

Kalas and Rich Ashburn made me feel very comfortable. It wasn't like I was taking someone's place. Byrum retired of his own volition, and they knew he was going to. They welcomed me. We had no problems whatsoever.

Baseball, it takes you a while to settle in . . . but after a few years, the fans develop a comfort level with you. Then after that, it's smooth sailing. Baseball is a daily soap opera, and the fans listen to it day after day after day, and it takes them a bit of time to get used to you.

I'll give you a story that exemplifies exactly what I'm talking about, that you can't please all people all the time. One day I was opening my mail, and I got a letter that said, "Andy, nice going. Congratulations. You're doing a great job. Keep giving those out-of-town scores. We really love them." The very next letter I opened started out, "You jerk." Right away I knew I was in trouble. "Don't bother with the out-of-town scores. All we want to hear is the Phillies game. Just stick to your knitting." Of course, that one was not signed. They were back-to-back examples: Now what are you going to do—give the scores, or not give the scores? In that case, you can't please any of the people some of the time if you don't go right down the middle. I don't know what the answer was.

The chemistry between Kalas and Ashburn was a broadcast sense of timing. Whitey was full of pauses and wasn't a professional announcer. Harry let him have his run, and they just meshed well together.

> The chemistry between Kalas and Ashburn was a broadcast sense of timing.

I knew that the Phillies were playing well during the stretch from 1976 to '83, and I knew that made it fun, and it also made it easier. But one day Harry came up to me—I don't know if it was late in '76 or late in '77—and he says, "Don't get used to this, pal. It's not always like this." He was right. By the time I got to the late '80s and the '90s, I had a bunch of bad seasons.

Even today, people recall to me my call of Mike Schmidt's East Division–winning homer in Montreal in 1980 (i.e., "He buried it") to me. That just shows how stupid I was, not to use it again. Harry was known for "It's outta here" because he was imitating Larry Bowa around the batting cage. Here I pulled that thing out and was too dumb to ever use it again.

In the early days, when the players weren't making as much

money as they are now and you were younger—more their age—you were, in a sense, on a par with them. But as the years went by and they started to make their millions and started to have their entourage while you were getting older and they were staying the same age, relatively, it became more of a difficult situation to deal with. There were always guys on the team you could go to. Maybe you didn't fool with some of them. Other guys were withdrawn. Other guys were much more outgoing. In fact, you could almost recognize the ones that someday wanted to be broadcasters, like Tim McCarver. He was especially cordial. Of course, he was a Southern gentleman to begin with.

There's a story that sounds apocryphal; it must have been one Harry told, which means it's probably true. He was until the end the MC of the Philadelphia Sportswriters' Dinner, which is held in a hotel in New Jersey. It's a big night, with a lot of out-of-town guests. The Phillies and other organizations would rent a suite, where you could party, before and after.

One year Harry was also the MC of the Phillies' caravan, which would visit area cities. The story goes that after he got through with his MC duties at the banquet, he made the round of parties. He was a pretty big party guy in his younger days. The story is, he got to his room, called the front desk and said, "This is Harry Kalas. I'd like to have a wakeup call for 6:30"—because the bus was leaving at 7. The operator said, "I'd be glad to do that, but I'd like you to know that it's 6 o'clock right now."

I remember distinctly one day in Cincinnati. It was a Sunday afternoon game and we had played a Saturday afternoon game, so he had the whole night to do what he was going to do. And he showed up Sunday when we were down on the field to tape our TV opening. Harry had sunglasses on, which he never wore for the opening. He had these dark sunglasses on. I said, "Harry, what are you doing with sunglasses on?" He said, "This is to protect the viewing public."

A VISIT TO PLANET McCARVER

Tim McCarver

Tim McCarver, 67, began his broadcast career with the Phillies in 1980, after his 21-year career as a major league catcher came to an end. He has been in the booth ever since, and currently serves as the analyst on Fox Sports' major league telecasts, a role he has held since 1996.

The first thing you think about when you think of Harry is his voice. I think of the fun we had when I worked for the Phillies in **'80***, '81 and '82. Everybody realized that Harry was the main voice of the broadcast. Of course, 1980 was my first year, so I was all ears and all eyes that year, in particular. I deferred salary my last two years of playing to see if I would be any good at broadcasting. I really had no idea what the business was all about, so I was very dependent on Harry, Chris Wheeler, Andy Musser and Whitey to show me the ropes . . . It's a business you have to learn quickly, and learning the rudiments of the business from somebody like Harry, was a real privilege.

Almost everything that first year caught me off-guard . . . I understood that the art of interviewing—pregame show, postgame show, all the stuff that I would be thrown into—was more difficult than the professionals made it appear. It was all new to me, and I was very serious about it, because I thought I could do it, but I didn't know. When you're on the other end of the interviews, answering questions about the game that you played for a long time, it's a lot easier. I was under no illusions that the

---

* *Sports Illustrated* rated New York City circa 1966 as the worst time and place to be a sports fan. The Yankees, Knicks and Rangers finished last, the Mets escaped last place for the first time and the Giants were 1–12–1. The best time and place to be a sports fan? Philadelphia, <u>1980</u>.

business was a piece of cake. I was dependent on guys—timing, rhythm, cadence, all of that stuff that I know a lot about now, because I've been doing it for 30 years. But I didn't have any idea then what the business was about. I had a tendency to talk too much and was a little overzealous. I felt like I had something to say, but finding the spots to say it is really what I learned and developed into my own style, I guess. But I learned it from Harry and Whitey and Wheels and Andy.

The one thing Whitey told me early was, "I learned a long time ago that if you don't have anything to say, don't say it." That made a lot of sense. Somebody told Whitey that early in his career, and that made an impact later on, when I started working for the networks, more than it did then. Because I was so enthusiastic, I was going to tell the world my version of baseball, at the risk of talking too much, not really knowing the timing and cadence and rhythm of the business.

And Whitey and Harry had a marvelous rapport—a legendary rapport, in many ways. There was a lot of wit, a lot of humor, a lot of wisdom, but it was the quintessential listening to two of your friends talk about the game. Everyone has said before that and since then, that that makes the best broadcast—if you as a viewer or you as a listener are listening to two of your favorite guys talk about something that you really like. To have the game brought to you the way they brought it to you has turned into legendary status. I don't think Harry and Whitey originally had the rapport that they had from 1980 on. That's just my opinion. Good partners get better, and you become more comfortable later on. I don't think long-ago St. Louis Cardinals' announcers Jack Buck and **HARRY CARAY*** had any rapport on radio in St. Louis until

*In 1949, **HARRY CARAY**'s first wife Dorothy divorced him. In 1979 Harry wrote her: "Dearest Dorothy, Enclosed is my 360th alimony check. How much longer is this _ _ _ going to continue?" Dorothy responded: "Dearest Harry, Til death do us part. Love, Dorothy." Harry paid monthly till he passed away in Palm Springs in 1998.

after Jack Buck left for two years—1959–60. Then when he came back, Harry realized what a great partner Jack Buck was, and they worked much, much better from 1961 on; Harry was fired in 1969.

Broadcasters are—and I hate to use that expression—much like wine: They do get better with age, and they do grow on you, and you do become more comfortable in listening to them. And the more you listen to them, the better they become. At that time Harry and Whitey had worked together eight or nine years.

Kalas had that connection with the fans because of Richie, in large part. Not that Harry ever shared his identity with Richie, but Harry was very fortunate to have had Richie for a partner, and likewise—Richie was very fortunate to have Harry as a partner. They complemented in style so terrifically. Now, is that to say that Harry lost something when Richie died in 1997? I don't think so, because by that time he had cemented his style with the Philadelphia fans. Had Richie died in 1973 instead of 1997—you never know—but I'm not too sure Harry would have been as popular with the fans as he turned out ultimately to be. But by working with Whitey for 28 years, it stands to reason that Harry's style was cemented in the Philadelphia baseball psyche.

> I was drawn to broadcasting because I did countless interviews in place of Steve Carlton . . .

There's some truth to the fact that I was drawn to broadcasting because I did countless interviews in place of Steve Carlton, who did not speak to the media for most of his time with the Phillies. All the writers came to me in those days. All I was doing was answering the questions. I wasn't using them to get a job. I was answering the questions because that's what I always did in St. Louis. I don't know that that's why I got the job, but I'm sure it didn't hurt, when Bill Giles decided to hire me.

That hiring took place in 1977. I had had a good year in '76, and the Toronto Blue Jays called me and asked if I'd sign a four-year deal to broadcast. They'd just come into existence, and they wanted me to broadcast up there. Giles heard about that, and he said, "Here's what we'll do: We'll give you whatever you want to play next year, and then we'll sign a two-year deal for television when you finish your career." So really, in effect, it was a three-year deal. I said OK. I ended up playing three more years, and during that time I answered questions about Lefty because he wasn't doing it, and I would imagine—I don't know; I can't speak for Bill—that he would think he made the right move.

I thought I might want to get into broadcasting, but a lot of guys think they might want to do it. Then they get in it, and it's a lot more difficult than they think it is. Or they have more name value, or something like that. Jim Palmer's a Hall of Famer, and he's been a broadcaster for a long time. Obviously I'm not a Hall of Famer, but I did pay attention to the game, and I paid attention to the people who taught me the game.

There are many things that are difficult about broadcasting. If it were that easy, there would be more qualified people doing it, and staying on for longer periods of time. It's learning that when you speak, it's important for people to listen, and they listen more when you have something to say—instead of just talking to fill air. And that's something I've learned later in my career. But that's something that Whitey certainly knew, and he broadcasted in that fashion. When Whitey said something, then usually people's ears perked up. That was part of the chemistry that Richie and Harry had, as everybody in Philadelphia knows.

I was really the fifth broadcaster in a four-man team. That's how I would describe my existence there in the broadcasting booth in Philadelphia. Then Wheels and I did the two-man booth with PRISM, a Philadelphia cable outlet; we did 30 games a year in '80, '81 and '82. I was just trying to fit in and do whatever I could. I kidded in a *New York Times* article after Harry's death that I was relegated to getting chairs for everybody that first year.

One night in Montreal Harry and I did the first three innings on radio, and then I was to join Whitey in the fourth inning. At old Olympic Stadium in Montreal, we see in the third inning this scorecard blowing down from the rafters . . . Somebody lost their scorecard. Well I go over in the fourth inning, and it was Whitey who lost his scorecard. He's doing play-by-play for an inning, and he has no scorecard. He's got to rely on his memory. It's tough to do a game without a scorecard, particularly the second time around. You know who's hitting and all that, but the second time through the lineup, you don't know in an instant what the guy did his prior at-bat. So Whitey says, "I'll get the game off your

> "Whitey, I'm not keeping score so you can read it. I'm keeping score so I can read it."

scorecard." I said all right—of course. I was the analyst, of course, and Whitey's doing play-by-play. He can't read my scorecard. Everybody keeps score the way they want to. Whitey screwed up everything, for the whole inning. And after the inning he says, "How in the world is anybody supposed to read your ------- score-card?" I said, "Whitey, I'm not keeping score so you can read it. I'm keeping score so I can read it." He said, "Well, I guess you're right." Typical Ashburn style.

I remember a ton of stories and a ton of things that happened when I worked with Ashburn, but I can't remember nearly as many when I worked with Harry. Harry didn't have Whitey's humor. Nobody did. Nobody was like Whitey. That's why Harry and Whitey were so good. I mean, Harry had the pipes, and Whitey had the humor, and they blended together into a fabulous team.

A lot of times when Ashburn didn't say anything on the air, he was opening his mail. That's a fact . . . I listen to tapes all the time, whether it's on television or radio or what have you, and sometimes you'd hear this letter opener going through a bill or letter or fan mail or whatever it was, and you'd hear in the background this distant echo of Whitey saying, "I already paid that." It was classic. I don't think anybody's ever done that.

Whitey he loved the 76ers, and he'd have a different monitor turned on so he could watch the 76ers while the Phillies were playing. And sometimes you'd hear, "Ohhhh . . ." when nothing was happening during the Phillies game. What had happened was, Dr. J had been fouled without a call, and Whitey thought it was a foul. He was marveling over a Sixers play, when nothing was happening with the Phillies. It was hilarious, and nobody could get away with that but Whitey.

Who was to know in 1980 that that would be the first World Series victory for the Phillies? I guess I was very fortunate. Fate dealt me a lucky hand along those lines. I can hear Harry calling those games against Houston in the National League Championship Series—particularly the one play that happened with Vern Ruhle, who was pitching for the Astros in Game Four, and **DOUG HARVEY***, who was the home plate umpire. And he had to go to National League president **CHUB FEENEY***. The game was delayed for 20 minutes, for Doug Harvey to determine what that play was. It could have been a triple play . . . It was ruled a double play. It was a very unusual play. I was on with Harry at the time; I was doing one inning on television, and Whitey had moved over to radio . . . But Harry's recapitulation of what had happened, was just brilliant. I remember him saying, "We are trying to be objective," because I thought it was a ridiculous call. I didn't think he caught the ball in the air, and that's the way it was ultimately ruled. But Harry kept saying, in his inimitable way, "We are trying to be objective here." Obviously, that was to counter my seeming subjectivity in going over the analysis.

Being close to the players may have been the case with Harry and Whitey, and it may be the case with the majority of the announcers, but that was never the case with me. In New York, in fact, I was fired for that reason in 1998, after doing Mets games for 16 years . . . It was never my style to get too chummy with the

***DOUG HARVEY** and **CHUB FEENEY** both appeared on "Jeopardy" . . . several years apart . . . the only baseball people to do so.

players, but Harry loved that particular part of it. And the players loved it. Harry was successful with it. Some guys deem it as part of their jobs to be close to the players. Other people think that being objective and always being factual and telling the truth is more important. It's hard to be both. It's not right or wrong; it's a matter of why people tune in. Your responsibility is to the people who are listening, not to the players. But there are some announcers who think their first responsibility is to the players. Players don't pay your salary. The people who listen to you do. There are many ways to be successful in this business, and it depends on a particular style. Harry had a style that endeared him to players, as much as the fans. And it worked. Who's to say what the right way is to do it? I don't think there is a right or a wrong way. It's your way.

Harry was very close to the guys. I'm not so sure he sugarcoated it on the air. But perhaps the best way to do a local broadcast is to infer or imply that you would prefer for the team to win, and there was a heavy inference on Harry's part that he would prefer that the Phillies won. No, he didn't sugarcoat it, but by intonation he showed fans that he was happier, and therefore they should be happier, if the Phillies won. Harry's marvelous intonation and tone, it was very powerful to the Philadelphia populace—without even telling them that he was doing it—but almost subconsciously he was saying, "If you pay attention to my voice, you'll know whether the Phillies are winning or not." That was the connection he had built. I'm not even too sure that the fans knew that.

The very fact that Harry is the only guy who has ever uttered the middle name of a home run hitter on his 500th home run—"Michael Jack Schmidt"—that was endearing when he did that, no question.

OF MIKES AND MEN

Curt Smith

A 1973 graduate of SUNY at Geneseo—Curt Smith is the author of eleven books, including Voices of Summer. *He has been a speechwriter for Presidents George H. W. Bush and Ronald Reagan. Of Curt Smith, Bob Costas says, "Curt stands up for the beauty of words."* USA Today *says, "He shows that broadcasting can be art." Currently, Smith hosts the weekly perspectives series on Rochester, New York's NPR affiliate, WXXI. He is a senior lecturer at the University of Rochester. He has appeared on numerous local and network radio/TV programs, including* Nightline *and ESPN's* SportsCenter.

Meeting Harry, you would say that his face belongs in the Vienna Boys Choir. Then, he opens his mouth. The voice is astonishing. It evoked, I always thought, a bass or lead cello or a wrecker raising cars. Bill Conlin, the great sportswriter, called it a 'four-Marlboro-into-a-three-martini-lunch baritone.' It was a voice impossible to ignore . . . impossible to forget. He played it like Yasha Heifetz did a violin. I mourn that, and, moreover, I mourn Harry because he was a friend, someone who entranced the Delaware Valley and swelled the Phillie Nation. That's quite a legacy.

Growing up in upstate New York, I was able to hear Harry do games. I really got to hear him and appreciate him after I moved to Washington, as a speechwriter in the early 1980s. Philadelphia is two and a half hours from Washington. I had relatives in West Chester—a Philadelphia suburb—and many weekends, I would get in the car and go to their house and sit on the back porch and listen to Harry. I had a lot of company because people tell stories of Brooklyn in the 1940s and early '50s. You could walk down the street without a radio and hear Red Barber from a hundred different directions. That's how it was with Harry. You could go into a bar—which I know he would appreciate—into a store, driving down the street and hear Harry from radios passing you. It was impossible to miss. He truly did mix—it seems to me—and knit Eastern Pennsylvania, Western New Jersey and Delaware.

In baseball, the rule is that you must talk a great deal, because in a three-hour game the ball may be in play for all of eight to nine minutes. You'd better be able to fill dead air or you'll have dead and expired audience.

Harry was different. The voice was so prepossessing, so commanding, he didn't need to talk as much as the average announcer. He had rather a Spartan style rhetorically. He did not intersperse anecdotal play-by-play as often as did other announcers. It didn't matter with him. He didn't need it. He had this marvelous instrument from the guy upstairs. Harry's voice was proof that God is indeed a baseball fan.

In this free-agent era—the buy-a-player era—the broadcaster is the umbilical cord, the connecting tissue between the game and the public. Players come and go, often within several years, often within the same season. They're in transit. They're ephemeral. Only the announcer lasts. Harry, for example, broadcast from 1971 through 2008 for the Phillies. Name me one player, even Michael Jack Schmidt, who was a Phillie for remotely that long. They don't exist.

Vin Scully, now in his 60th year of broadcasting for the Dodgers, is the link between **EBBETS FIELD*** and Chavez Ravine. I could go on and on, but the point is that announcers come and "don't" go. If they're good enough—if they last long enough—they become an extended member of the family. That's what Harry became. He became not simply a member of the Phillies—he headed the Phillies family.

> *Only 6,700 fans attended the Dodgers' finale at **EBBETS FIELD** in 1957. The park—built 44 years earlier—had a capacity of 32,000 with only 700 parking spaces. An apartment building now sits on that site.

The second point is a broadcaster like Harry who did every game on radio and, increasingly, on television did 162 games a year. He did exhibition games. If the postseason arose, for example, last year, he would do probably a dozen games in postseason with the Phils. Add it together and you're talking about almost 200 games a year. The average game now lasts three hours, sadly. Add pre-game and post-game, and you're talking about 800 hours a year. How many hours are in a week? 168. So, you're talking about a broadcaster who literally spends five weeks a year, solid, 24-7 with you. How could you not become enamored of someone like that? You know the broadcaster, although you've maybe never met him, as well as—or better than—your Uncle Fred or Aunt Ethel. That's why it matters more. Not simply the players, but why they matter more than broadcasters in any other sport.

In 1987 I wrote *Voices of the Game*. I began it in 1984. No one had ever written a book like this. It has been called the "definitive history of baseball broadcasting." The first baseball game ever broadcast was on KDKA in Pittsburgh in 1921. It turned out to be a much more exhaustive project than I had envisioned. It's more than 600 pages, in large part because it is such a seductive subject matter and also because all of it was virginal.

In 2005 I wrote *The Voices of Summer*. This is a book I began with some trepidation because I didn't wish to be presumptive. I was ranking the best 101 broadcasters among the more than 1,000 who have done the game. I concocted what I thought—and think—was a very fair criterion, a point scale of what makes a great announcer each on a one-to-ten point scale—the perfect announcer therefore would get 100 points. Guess what? Vin Scully is the perfect announcer! He got 100. I didn't want to make him perfect because only one person is perfect, and He's upstairs. But I could not not do that. He's what I call the Roy Hobbs of baseball broadcasting. Then, the next one

> I was ranking the best 101 broadcasters among the more than 1,000 who have done the game.

was in 2007: *The Voice, Mel Allen's Untold Story*, a story of triumph, tragedy, and then a revival he had. He lost all and then came back. He was the most famous sportscaster in the country. And then, at the age of 51, Mel Allen fell off the cliff. He went into eclipse. He became an MIA, a nonperson for decades. This book sought to understand why. In essence, to discover why the most recognizable voice in the country was silenced for more than a decade.

> The grammar and language heard on the air today, particularly by ex-jocks, is appalling.

The grammar and language heard on the air today, particularly by ex-jocks, is appalling. It's very sad for the age and culture in which we live. "You scream loudly, so therefore, you are heard." The more profane you are, the more hip you become with a cutting edge. All these stupid moronic bromides that masquerade as thought today. In our schools, we don't teach English. We don't encourage our kids to read. We don't encourage them to read the classics. We don't talk about how sinful it is to have prepositions that conclude a sentence, or participles that dangle, or tenses that split. What do we do instead? We allow our kids to play these imbecilic video games, to use the computer instead of accessing something called "a book" in something called "a library." Our popular culture, by definition, is no better or worse than the culture itself.

I don't think Harry Kalas would have been the big-time announcer he became without that voice. I don't think there's any question about that, but it's impossible to separate the voice from the man. Mel Allen would not have been the household name he was without that voice. Edward R. Murrow would not. The voice, particularly on radio, is exceedingly important because after all it's all you have. Ernie Harwell once said to me, "On radio . . . until the announcer speaks . . . nothing has occurred." And he's right. This is certainly no criticism of Harry. Harry would be the first to agree that the voice was absolutely essential to his amazing success.

There are fine announcers, but none whose voice is so special, so unique as Harry's. People use the word "unique" and overuse the word "unique." Harry's voice was unique. There was quite literally nothing like it. It allowed him to prosper in baseball with a style that, with a lesser voice, would not have allowed him to become the nonpareil voice of NFL Films, and allowed him to do voice-overs—not saying a lot, just like baseball, but saying it with such élan and panache that it reached out and grabbed you, whether it was a Michael Jack Schmidt or Campbell's Soup. Harry was the perfect thespian.

Harry was a great practitioner of English. He used his voice as an instrument. He understood that this was his stock in trade. He understood why he was in such great demand. He took care of the voice, too. I think he would admit that he smoked and drank too much. He talked about that all the time. Except for that, I think he preserved his voice. I knew he was sick a couple of years ago. I have hosted for three or four years a series, "Voices of the Game," on XM Radio from the Baseball Hall of Fame. About two years ago, thank goodness, we honored Harry before it was too late. We honored him with an hour-long tribute Hall of Fame broadcast on XM. Several officials from the Hall and Harry and myself had dinner beforehand. Harry was rather quiet.

Over the last three or four years, the Hall has honored a number of Hall of Fame announcers. These are voices who have received the Ford C. Frick Broadcast Award, first given in 1978 to Mel Allen and Red Barber. Now it's given annually to one person.

It was hard for Harry to get away during the baseball season, but it was on a Saturday. The Hall had him driven from Philadelphia to **COOPERSTOWN*** and back. It was a series of one-hour tributes which I hosted. I had a stopwatch and we did 60 minutes for a 60-minute program. As I often said, it was akin to Ralph Edwards'

****COOPERSTOWN** (N.Y.) was named for the father of James Fennimore Cooper.

This is Your Life. That's what we did. We talked about him growing up in Naperville, Illinois, and going to school in Iowa, and going into the military. Then, of course, doing re-creations, and going to Houston and to Philadelphia. So, within 60 minutes, all done with that absolutely magnificent voice—the baritone which filled the room, filled the radio, filled the city, filled the Phillies Nation.

I was sitting there with Harry. I had told him beforehand, tongue-in-cheek, "Harry, I'm here, but you're carrying me." And he did, for 60 minutes. At the very end—I'll never forget it—I said, "I would be remiss if I didn't ask you to repeat your calling card." Of course, with that, no further introduction needed, he said as only Harry could, "We're outta here." What many people didn't realize about Harry was that he was very private, soft-spoken, introspective, which I admire and I admired in him. I liked him. I liked him a great deal and always had.

I do not think Harry overstayed his time. A lot of announcers do overstay. The old phrase, "they stayed too long at the fair." I'm not going to mention those who have stayed too long. You can tell when they start to make mistakes—losing track of where they are or what they're saying, repeating themselves, dead air, the timbre of the voice receding to a shadow of what it once was. Those are the traits which come to mind. I listened to Harry very closely and none of those traits seemed to excess.

Sarah Bernhardt had the line, "I retired at the top of my career." Harry died at the top of his career.

In 2005, when I wrote *Voices of Summer* I ranked Harry as 25th—that's 25th of more than 1,000 people who broadcast baseball. If I were to redo that book today—because longevity and continuity were two of the criteria—he would doubtless be in the top 10-15 broadcasters of all time. My top five, again, in 2005, were Vin Scully, Mel Allen, Ernie Harwell—nature's nobleman, Jack Buck and Red Barber.

To me, argument was the reason for the book. As I said in the introduction, "Baseball is the oldest and greatest talking game there is. At its center is debate, dialogue." Is DiMaggio better than Mantle? Is Duke Snider better than Willie Mays? Was Allen better than Barber? Was Harry Caray better than **BRICKHOUSE***? That is absolutely essential to the game's DNA. The book was very well received. Obviously the broadcasters who made the list were appreciative. Broadcasters who didn't make the list, but perhaps should have, were quite graceful as well. I was quite taken by that. There were really only two broadcasters whose names of course will remain unmentioned who expressed the view that they should have made that list.

We are constantly surprised—but should not be—by the orgy of grief that follows a broadcaster of his ilk's death. I think of Harry Caray in Chicago, where WGN literally televised the parade, had a blimp at the funeral procession. It was like the death of a president. And St. Louis at Jack Buck's death, same thing. The cortege was driven down the interstate and there were people by the thousands standing along the sides of the road. Why? Because he was an extended member of the family, even though most of them had never met Jack Buck. They thought they did . . . and, in a sense, they had. Same thing with Harry Kalas. I believe Harry's passing is the only time in baseball history, except for Babe Ruth's death, where literally the body lay in state at a ballpark and Jack Buck's in St. Louis. It was behind home plate and thousands on that Saturday morning paid their respects. Thousands—wearing Phillies hats—touched the casket, left flowers. If that's not a legacy, I don't know what is.

He was the poetry of baseball on the air, where you can go from a store to your convertible, to a car or to a bar or school, and the common denominator was Harry. The Voice of the Voice.

*For many seasons, Jack **BRICKHOUSE** was the TV announcer for both the Cubs and the White Sox. The teams would televise home games only. The first voice heard when WGN-TV went on the air in 1948 was that of Jack Brickhouse.

IF THE PHONE DOESN'T RING IT'S HARRY AND RICHIE

Ray Tipton

Ray Tipton joined the Phillies in 1983 and serves as the game director for the Phillies broadcasts. A consummate professional, Tipton was the man behind the camera for Harry Kalas' Phillies broadcasts for 26 years and won Emmys for his work.
He was immortalized in the book More than Beards, Bellies and Biceps: The Story of the 1993 Phillies, *when broadcaster Chris Wheeler recalled having to do interviews in the clubhouse while players hit him with pies and poured champagne and beer on him. As Wheeler tried to end the interviews amid this distress, he reported that Tipton was shouting into his earpiece, "Keep going! This is great stuff!"*

I'm not a native Philadelphian; I'm from the Midwest—**OHIO***. I had heard his voice a couple of times, so I knew him and I had certainly heard of him. I grew up watching the Cleveland Indians and Cincinnati Reds.

It's funny and interesting that when I met Harry for the first time, it was in the airport. I had worked for four years at ESPN before I took this job, so I had an idea about Harry but only what my imagination allowed. When I came to Philly, the first thing I did was travel around to the other National League cities to check

*In the 1976 Ohio State-Indiana Game, Indiana scored on the first play of the second quarter to take a 7-6 lead. Indiana coach, Lee Corso, called a timeout. During the timeout, Corso had his team pose for a group picture with the scoreboard—showing Indiana leading **OHIO** State 7-6—clearly visible in the background. Corso featured the picture on the cover of the 1977 Indiana recruiting brochure. Ohio State won the game 47-7.

out camera angles and the equipment in each ballpark to pre-pare. On one of those trips, I was in the airport and—I forget where I was going—I was in one of those waiting areas and all I heard was that voice.

Harry was right behind me talking to fans about what to expect that season. "Yeah, we had a tough year last year." "Glad you came out last year, and we promise to be better next year," and "We love the fans, your support means everything to us."

I couldn't believe it was him. I had never met him, but I knew I was going to be working with him and I just couldn't believe that he was right there. I even debated whether or not to introduce myself but I did and in typical Harry fashion he welcomed me from the start. He was very kind and considerate and very warm to me. It was an unusual meeting but it was perfect because of exactly who he was. That's how we met and he was just so easy to work with from the get-go.

> Harry always gave Whitey (Richie Ashburn) his time and he would lie in the weeds . . .

He told me at that first—I guess you can call it a meeting—"We understand you're new here. You tell us what you want and we'll try to deliver it for you." What boss ever says that? Just watching Harry work, he was very smooth and he never got rattled. If you wanted to change something, he would do it. He almost never questioned any decision or change we made. He did a lot of it on the fly because that's what happens on televi-sion. It was great for me because he made it easy for me. That was a gift of his, he made our jobs easier by just being the person he was.

Everybody knows that Harry was a laid-back broadcaster, but that didn't mean he wasn't a perfectionist. It was the perfect combination for what we needed. Harry always gave Whitey his time and he would lie in the weeds, let Whitey tell his story and then come back with a zinger. That was fine for me. I would try to compliment them if I could, like if I knew something was going on, on the field or with whatever they were saying. That's how we worked for years.

He would once in a while ask, "How does that fit in?" I'd tell him and he'd say "OK." I never had to write out a promo, he could just do it. Or, if I did write out a promo, he'd read it word for word. This is what I want and he'd say OK.

Rarely would he mess up. If he did, he would get aggravated, but the second time would be perfect. Actually, it was usually one try and that was it.

He wouldn't say, "I want to do something." He would rely on me and our crew, but if he disagreed he'd say something. But that rarely happened.

You know, it's funny that Harry loved to get Whitey talking about those **METS*** days—when Whitey played for them and they were awful. That's where Whitey wrapped up his career and, surprisingly, Whitey loved to talk about those years. I guess it was so bad he knew the stories were funny. Harry once said, maybe we shouldn't talk about the Mets so much because they are our competition, but my feeling was to just go with it. Everybody loved Whitey so much and the stories were so good that people would tell me that they loved those stories. You know, "Wally Post was called Wally Post because he ran like a post." He would tell the story about Casey Stengel walking up and down the dugout talking. "Here I have Mr. Ashburn if I want to steal a base. Here I have Mr. Post if I need to hit a home run."

Then there was the story of the ash **BAT***. When Whitey was on a

*After the **METS** had played their first nine games in their inaugural 1962 season, they were 9½ games out of first place.

*Orlando Cepeda used more **BATS** than any player in history. He felt each bat had exactly one hit in it. When Cepeda hit safely, he would discard the bat. He had 2,364 hits in his career.

hitting streak, he would take his bats to bed with him. Harry would lead him into it with "Wow, those must have been pretty good bats. What were they made of?"

"Ash," and it would always be ash from Maine or ash from New Hampshire.

And Harry would say, "How long have you had that bat?"

"I've had it a long time."

"That bat must be pretty special."

"Well, I've been to bed with a lot of old bats."

And you'd hear everyone laughing. The tech crew in the background would be laughing. That also had to do with the fact that Harry was so nice to the tech crews no matter where he went. He thought of them as our extended family, and they knew all the jokes as well. He was always very warm and thankful and grateful to them. A lot of people would ask him for their voicemail message. Actually, they'd come up to me first because they didn't want to bother him, but they wanted that "Outta here" call on their phone. Nobody realized that he loved doing that and never turned it down. Anyway, we were in **ST. LOUIS*** and one of the technicians asked me if he could ask Harry to do it. They were just timid about asking for something so . . . not trivial, but you understand what I mean. So I told him no problem, but if he wanted me to introduce him I would. So I told Harry that this cameraman was going to come up to him the next day and ask him to do this. Harry said no problem and then asked me about him and his life. So I gave Harry a little background, and I told him this guy was a huge fan of Harry's despite being a St. Louis fan and that he had recently gone through a divorce. The next

---

*All six games of the 1944 World Series were played at Sportsman's Park in **ST. LOUIS**. The rival managers—Luke Sewell of the Browns and Billy Southworth of the Cardinals—shared a one-bedroom apartment during the season . . . never expecting both teams to be in town at the same time.

day, I go in. "Harry, this is Tim, and he'd like you to do his message."

"Nice to meet you, Tim. Is there anything specific you want me to say?"

"No, whatever you do is great."

"This is Harry Kalas and Tim's not here right now. He's way, way outta here like a 3-0 pitch to Jack Clark. And, he's probably not coming back."

That's referring to his divorce and everyone is laughing. Harry tries to do a real one and the guy says, "No, I love that one." That was Harry, he tried to personalize everything. That day, as always happened, three or four people left the booth happy just because Harry was Harry.

I miss him. I miss the little things. I miss him because he was so steady, you knew what you were going to get. You never worried about getting something done. I miss him on the plane and the little things he would say. Those little things are what you miss.

We'll Be Back Right After This

People would write in letters all the time: "Dear Mr. Kalas, my fiancée is the biggest Phillies fan ever, could you please do something for our wedding?" And he'd come up to me and say, "Brooksie, I've got another wedding announcement. When can we do this?" In the offseason, he'd come in every Wednesday to get his mail, and it never stopped. They'd just write to Harry Kalas, care of the Phillies. He'd open every letter, and he'd do every request. And the thing about Harry was, he'd always ask, "Brooksie, I've got a couple wedding announcements in the mail. Can we do another one?"

I don't ever remember seeing him acting like he didn't feel like it, or acting like it was an imposition. It was automatic. If the fans asked, how could he not?

When we'd have our ALS function, which is an autograph party and a charity auction, without fail the last table would be Harry's table. Every time. The team always has that ALS party on a getaway day, so we'd leave as soon as it was over. Every time we'd be assembled at the bus, and it would be: "Where's Harry?" The answer was always the same: "He's still signing."

He takes every picture. He talks to everybody. Every single year, without fail, people were still there, lined up, waiting for Harry. Everybody got a conversation. He always felt like he owed them more than just an autograph.

When I first started, I didn't know Harry Kalas. I mean, I knew of him—everybody did—but I didn't know him personally. It was the 1993 season, and the first few times he referred to me, he called me Michael Brooks. And I knew why—Michael Brooks was a basketball player at LaSalle, and Harry had done some Big Five games. It was really no big deal for me. But once at the end of a broadcast, as he's thanking all the people who worked that day, he said: "And thanks to our engineer Michael Brooks"—and he caught himself. And he had this really mad look on his face. He just looked grim; it grieved him that he'd done that. And he said:

"Oh, your name's not Michael." We're on the air, now! We're still on the air. And he said: "Your name's not Michael, it's Robert Brooks. I'm sorry, Brooksie. Folks, that's our engineer Robert Brooks."

He never shrugged off a mistake, and he cared so much about the people he worked with. He didn't take that stuff lightly. He didn't need to do that, but that's Harry. When I met him, he was a big-time announcer. But I never saw him big-league anybody. He treated everyone great.

Every once in a while, we'd go through the crowd out to Harry the K's, the restaurant in left field at Citizens Bank Park. I just thought it was nice to make sure people saw Harry in Harry the K's every once in a while. But the thing with Harry was, you had to allot extra time whenever you went anywhere with him. Most guys when they're moving through a crowd develop The Walk—"Hey, nice to see you, gotta go, take care, good to see you, gotta go . . . " but Harry always stopped. He engaged everyone. He always seemed happy that anyone wanted to talk with him— and they always did.

—**Rob Brooks**, Phillies manager of broadcasting

Obviously the 4:41 in the morning thing resonates, because as a closer, you don't get many opportunities to get a hit at 4:41 in the morning . . . I didn't pitch in the first game, and I got brought in in the ninth of a tie game in the second game. Ended up I threw the ninth and the 10th, and manager Jim Fregosi came to me after I pitched the 10th and said, "You're not going back out there to pitch, but if it gets to you in the order, you've got to hit. You're up fourth. I'm out of guys." So I went up there to the plate, and did the only thing I know how to do—swing hard and hope Hoffman hit my bat.

Probably the thing that sticks with me the most is on the replay of that game. Harry says to Ashburn on the broadcast, "Three-thirty in the morning, Your Whiteness." And Whitey says, "Just the shank of the evening for you, Harry." They were awesome together. Moments like that are what made them special. That's what made the people in Philadelphia love them, because they could just be two guys in a bar talking.

When we clinched, when we beat Atlanta to go to the World Series, that call was memorable—and the shock in Harry's voice, that I actually retired a team in a 1-2-3 inning.

I don't think it's any secret—'93 was Harry's favorite team. If you look at it, there were 25 guys on that team who could have just as easily been digging a ditch. Harry felt real comfortable around that. No one put on airs whatsoever. It wasn't about being a big-league baseball player. We were just guys that were lucky enough to be given a job to play a game. And Harry always viewed himself as being lucky enough to sit there and call a game, and do what he loved to do. So there was that kinship. And heck, he was in the back of the plane with us, playing cards every trip. We just clicked together—Harry and all of us players were the same kind of people.

Harry was the best. He was a guy that wasn't media. Whatever he did, no one on the team ever considered him media. He was just part of the team.

What Harry did, just the way he brought the game to people, you either have it or you don't. It's not something that can be forced. He just had a way of telling you what was happening on the field. He could actually paint the picture for you when he was on radio, and when he was on TV, he brought it all to life. He just had one of those voices. He was the voice of every person in Philadelphia, really.

He connected to the fans because he never acted like he was anything other than one of them. Harry, to put it bluntly, was the stuff in Philadelphia. He never considered himself that. He was just a guy. It didn't matter what your lot in life was, Harry didn't consider himself any better than that person. He was just a guy that had a great voice.

—**Mitch Williams**, former pitcher,
current studio analyst for the MLB Network

In the early days of my career I came across Harry, and he was always very, very helpful. I would ask him for help; I thought my career was stalled. He would listen to me and tell me I was doing all the right things, that I had the ability and I should be patient. If I kept doing what I was doing, it would happen. It was only a matter of time.

He wasn't a guy to force advice on you: "I'm a superstar, let me help poor little old you." He treated everybody well. He never acted like a big shot. He was as nice to me as he was a network star. Harry treated everybody the same, and he was extremely approachable.

I'm doing a book on sports broadcasting, and on Feb. 3 I sat down with Harry at the Newtown Grill. He talked about his life, broadcasting and philosophy. He told me he got his "outta here" call from former Phillies shortstop Larry Bowa. It was funny—we were sitting and talking in the grill, and the fans would stop at the table. They were shocked to see the two of us together.

Occasionally Harry would take a trip with the Eagles. He was doing the game for Westwood One radio network, and he would get permission to hop on the charter. We would always chat. When we would do that, people would always want to take our picture together. He would always ask about my kids and my family. I would ask about Todd, Harry's eldest son.

—**Merrill Reese**, 66, the longtime play-by-play voice of the Philadelphia Eagles

The lasting image I'll have of him was in Clearwater this year. He had some health problems, and he didn't get down there until the middle of March. It was the last Sunday, it was against Boston, and he was there because it was a TV game.

My wife Lori was there. After the game, we went to see a couple friends at the Tiki Bar. We were there for a short while, and my wife had a flight out, so we're making our way out to the parking lot. We're walking out the back steps to the car, and on the back half-field, on the side of the fence, there's Harry. He's all alone. On the other side of the fence, there must have been 200 fans—all wanting an autograph or a handshake, or a conversation. All the fans on the other side saw him, and they all came running around. And he's there, he's signing every autograph, and he doesn't leave until he's talked to everybody there.

I wished I had a camera. It's late afternoon, and the sun is going down. He's done the broadcast. He's done. He can go home. It's been a long day, I'm sure he's tired. But there he is, signing hundreds of autographs because people wanted to see him, and he's going to take care of every single one of them. I've said this a lot lately—that's the one thing that always comes to my mind when I think of Harry. That moment.

He's already in the Hall of Fame. He's got the absolutely tremendous last call of a World Series on his resume. He's made a friend of every fan in his great career. He's done everything anybody ever needs to do. He doesn't have to stand there and sign autographs; at this point in his career if Harry had said, "Folks, I'm tired, I've been in the booth all day, I'd like to go home and get some rest"—or whatever gracious thing he might have said—I'm sure everybody would have been OK with it. But that's not the guy he was. He was going to make sure he was there to the end, he took care of everyone, he granted whatever request they had.

Harry taught me a lot of lessons in the time we spent together. I didn't know him that long; I had a grandfatherly relationship with him. But that's a lesson that I will always remember—those people on the other side of the fence, they're why we do this job. Without them, there's no reason for us. Harry never lost sight of that. He never lost sight of why he was doing it—to make the fans happy.

—**Scott Franzke**, commentator for Phillies radio broadcasts

When I took the job in New York, Harry was one of the first people to call me. He knew how hard it was to leave, he knew how much I loved it here, but he also knew it was a better opportunity. And when I got a chance to come back, Harry was one of the first people to call me to welcome me back. He really made it easy, telling everybody I was such a good, young broadcaster and what a great addition I'd be. He didn't have to do that, but that was Harry. In a million little ways, Harry always made you comfortable in his environment.

When I left for New York, I asked him if he had any advice. Harry knew all about replacing a popular figure because he always said when he replaced Bill Campbell it was really hard for him at first. He said, "Just be patient. Be patient. Let them get to know you. You'll be fine, T-Mac."

Nobody replaces Harry. Harry can't be "replaced;" it's not the right word.

I'm not sure he ever called me "Tom." It's always "T-Mac." When Harry puts a nickname on you, that's it. My son was playing in a baseball tournament in Delaware, and everybody was calling him "T-Mac."

For the memorial service at the ballpark, I got here really early since I was the master of ceremonies. I wanted to see everyone come in, to watch all the people walk by. This place is so big, but it felt so intimate that day. It was like an auditorium that fit everybody perfectly. The video on the scoreboard was on a loop; it started over every half hour. And at every point, the crowd reacted the same way, at the same scene they'd already watched several times. The way they cheered every one of Harry's calls on that tape, that was the way they said goodbye to him.

I was in a position where I'm looking at the crowd the whole time. I loved watching the expression on people's faces—seeing Rich Ashburn smile at something, seeing Bill Giles' face light up, seeing the fans laugh. That was all I could think of—this gigantic place became so intimate, you could grasp everything that everybody was going through. It was tremendous. It was unbelievable.

I was nervous because of the magnitude of it. We wanted to do it the way Harry would have wanted us to do it—he'd want us to laugh, and he'd want us to celebrate. And everybody, in their own way, it sure felt like they did.

—**Tom McCarthy**, Phillies announcer, 2001–05, 2008–present; Mets announcer 2006–07

I did some radio last year when they'd give Scott Franzke the day off. After Harry had eye surgery, I happened to be doing his first game back. It was really a big thrill for me—that I got to introduce him and welcome him back to the booth. A huge thrill.

Well, what I didn't know was, Harry holds the play-by-play announcer responsible for how the team plays in his absence. If you were filling in for him, and the team didn't play well, it was your fault. And he'd give you the Harry Kalas wave—kind a disdainful brush-off wave, with a disgusted look on his face.

On this day, Cole Hamels is pitching and the Phillies lead the Braves 3-0 when I enter the booth. Harry said to me: "You think you can handle this?" I'm thinking I've got Cole Hamels on the mound, I'm feeling pretty good about things. Well, Cole gives up nine runs. He threw a ball into centerfield, it was horrible. Keystone Cops. And I'm thinking, *Oh my God, he's going to kill me when he comes back in.*

I purposely didn't make eye contact with him. I wouldn't even look at him. But Harry just stood next to me until I looked up—and as soon as he caught my eye he gave me the wave.

Then Harry sits back down—and they score seven runs for Harry! They get four straight hits, Greg Dobbs hits a home run, they take the lead. And Harry never said a word. He just looked at me, and then he looked at the scoreboard and shrugged with a big smile on his face. The Phillies held on to win 10-9—and that was the day I got the Harry Wave.

When Harry made the call of the final out in the 2008 World Series, I was right next to him. The shot you see of Harry at that moment, I'm right behind the camera. That's every announcer's dream, to get that chance—to call the championship moment. I know how bad Harry wanted that, because he didn't get that chance in 1980. And now I'm sitting next to this icon at the penultimate moment of his career.

I felt so proud for so many people that day. But I couldn't have felt better for anyone than I felt for Harry Kalas. I don't know if you can tell from the video when you look at it, but I could see that there were tears in his eyes as he's making that call. And he nailed the call. Just perfect. That is a moment I will never forget because I know what it meant to him.

During the parade, I'm with the Phillies broadcasters. Pat Burrell was sitting in the first car when he jumped onto the firetruck. But we were really the first float in that thing, all of us riding in the parade. And the noise . . . all you could hear were chants of "Harry! Harry! Harry!" just booming, the sound bouncing back at you off the buildings. It was like going into the Roman Coliseum. I'd never heard anything like it.

It was a Harry lovefest. And he kept moving from side to side on our float. He wanted to make eye contact with every person there. That day no one got more cheers than Harry Kalas.

Harry has always tried to low-key the way the fans feel about him. But that moment, the reality of it really hit him. That was a moment when he could really feel just how beloved he was. And there was no question—he was absolutely flabbergasted by it. The fans got that chance to show him how they felt about him. And believe me, there were tears in his eyes the whole time.

—**Jim Jackson**, author, voice of the Flyers

For whatever reason, we were in Detroit and I was just wandering through the airport and I see Harry there. I'm from Boston, so I only knew him for a year. He called me over and unbelievably he started asking me about hockey and the Flyers. Things like did I play juniors or high school and how he could never do hockey and how Gene Hart was terrific. I kept trying to steer the conversation away from hockey to baseball but he kept coming back to hockey. It was like he knew me his whole life and I had only met him briefly at banquets, on the field or in the press box. I couldn't believe he knew me. I don't know if he was truly interested or just trying to make me comfortable. I don't know how but he got it out of me that I played squash and every time I saw him after that he tried to get me to play Whitey in squash. I had no interest because I knew Ashburn was at a higher level.

There are very few people in this world you can meet and right away feel comfortable with. I'm not awed by anybody but to feel that comfortable immediately, that's a rare gift.

—**Al Morganti**, 610 WIP Morning Show

Harry Kalas and Jack Buck were my best friends. Both Harry and I went to the University of Iowa and always had that in common. Every time we saw each other—spring training season, his ballpark or my ballpark—Harry always came in with an Iowa cheer that went "EE-OH-A-WAH-WAH," and Harry would then say "Hawkeye, how have you been doing?" We'd talk about whatever season was going on. We always compared our notes about the Iowa football team and Iowa basketball team. Then we'd talk about how our ballclubs were doing. We were very close. It's unusual that two guys who graduated from Iowa are both in Cooperstown.

There's an advantage to being from the Midwest, because there's no accent. Look at all the number of people from **IOWA*** and the University of Iowa, WSUI, the number of successful people who came out of there and made it big, not only in sports, but in newscasting.

We also had another very common thread. When I was with the Pirates in '79, and we won the World Series, that was the year they stopped letting the local announcer do the games. I had a fit about it. I really popped off big time. Here I'd waited all this time to do a World Series, and ABC Television took over. Their announcers were Keith Jackson and Howard Cosell. Cosell, who didn't know the left-field foul pole from the suicide squeeze, didn't know anything about our players. I popped off pretty good. The next year, '80, Harry Kalas didn't get to do the World Series, and I don't think

---

*In 1939, the Heisman Trophy winner was Nile Kinnick of **IOWA**. He is the only Heisman Trophy winner to have his university's football stadium named after him. In 1934, Nile Kinnick was Bob Feller's catcher on an American Legion baseball team.

he popped off as much as I did, but he was hurt by it. It's just a crime that, even today, FOX doesn't let the local announcer come in and, if not share it, at least be a part of the broadcast so that the people around the country can hear the voices of the teams that are in the World Series.

When Harry got to Clearwater this spring, the ballpark he'd been in many, many times, he was asking, "How do I get to the press box?" He was more ill than people knew.

—**Milo Hamilton**, announcer, Houston Astros, 55 years as a big league announcer, in a record 57 parks

I did know of him because in Los Angeles we had the great Vin Scully and I knew that Harry was on the same level in Philadelphia that we held Vin in Los Angeles. Somebody made a point of introducing me to Harry when I got here. It was that important to everyone that I got to meet Harry. I never got to meet Whitey but I did get to meet Harry.

That first summer I arrived in Philly from Los Angeles Comcast wasn't on the air yet. We made our debut in October so I spent a lot of time at the ballpark just meeting people and getting familiar with the ballclub and the setting. One night I went into the pressroom to eat. It was the day of Whitey's funeral and Harry sat down across from me. On the TV behind me, they started re-airing the service. At that point, it was Harry's eulogy. Harry was watching it and he started crying. Here I am in front of this great broadcaster and Harry has tears streaming down his face. I asked if he wanted me to leave because I didn't want him to feel uncomfortable. He said no, no, and asked me to stay. Clearly that was a traumatic day for him. I didn't know at the time and a lot of people have told me since that a little bit of Harry died that day as well. I told a lot of people at the time, I really got to share something, albeit sad and heartbreaking, but it told me something about the man. He didn't look at me as someone he needed to push aside and from that moment on I had a great respect of Harry.

That day when Harry passed away I was in the studio preparing to do the pregame show. Someone came in and said be ready to go on because Harry collapsed. Obviously we didn't know the extent right away but we found out that it all unfolded very quickly. The next thing I knew, Ricky Bottallico and I are on the set and we broke into our programming and announced that Harry had passed away. We had Dan Baker on and he hadn't heard until we called him. We had Larry Shenk on, and everyone at one point or another broke down or cracked a little. I tried everything I could not to break down because I felt my job at that point was to allow everyone else to tell their story. I was there to guide people through what they had to say. We did four or five hours of live television around Harry. I was proud of what we were able to bring and to be able to broadcast from his funeral is an honor and at the same time difficult to embrace because it's a moment that seems so personal but it's also professional. Here's a moment that's so private and personal and yet we were able to bring it to people who loved Harry and that was an honor. Michael Barkann and I were on for three straight hours and we cried during the broadcast. I thought that was OK because it was the same way everybody was feeling. I was so glad they didn't pull the cameras up on us when they played "Bridge Over Troubled Waters" because we were a mess. Now that it's over, the healing process has begun and people are telling stories with a smile on their face.

—**Leslie Gudel**, Comcast Sportsnet Philadelphia

When I was at Glassboro State College (now Rowan University), I interned at Channel 6 in Philadelphia. We were able to get press credentials and go to the ballpark every once in a while. One day in my junior year, I went down to the field and happened to get there as the Phillies finished taping their pregame show. I was the Sports Director at WGLS-FM and hosted a weekly talk show, and really wanted some big-name guests. Harry was always one of my favorites. I introduced myself and asked him to be a guest, and he said he'd be happy to do it. In my opinion, it was a great hour of sports talk radio. After he came on, I worked up the nerve to ask if he'd mind listening to my demo tape and give me some pointers. I really wanted to break into the business and valued his opinion. He said he'd be more than happy to.

Within a week of sending him the tapes, he sent me a nice letter with some suggestions. I was really taken aback by the fact that, here I was a 20-year-old college kid, and Harry Kalas took the time to listen to my tape, and really try to help me. Some of the things he pointed out I still use when I'm doing play-by-play. One of the first things he told me was always give the score every couple of minutes, so there's a Harry Kalas timer that goes off in my head. I still have that letter; I'll never get rid of it.

"Dear Ed,

I received the tapes, had a chance to listen to them, and they sound good. I appreciate the fact that they were not in audition tape form. When you put one together for an audition, you should put about two or three minutes of your best football or basketball, and maybe a portion of your interview with Tug McGraw.

Your basketball was good. It had all the ingredients and I knew where the ball was, who had it and the score. Good recognition of the personnel. The interview with Tug was great. It always helps to have a great subject, which Tug is, but your questions were excellent. The excitement of football was good. The recognition of the players was good. After Glassboro's first interception before the half, you mention that Glassboro took a time out to stop the clock, but no mention of how many remained after that. Try to keep track of each team's time outs and how many remain . . . After each score, give the score. You can never give the score enough. Had I just tuned in, I would have known that Glassboro had just scored, but not what the game score was at the time. After the second interception prior to the half, you mention there was a penalty on the play and then said, 'Glassboro would have a first down at the 29-yard line,' then had to come back and say, the ball would be brought back into Profs' territory. Don't set down the yard marker until you have sorted out the penalty.

All of your tapes are pretty good. You have good enthusiasm and good working knowledge of the games you are calling. You are getting great experience at Glassboro, that I'm sure will pay off when you get out into this wonderful world of professional sportscasting.

Very best to you.
Sincerely, Harry Kalas."

Amazing. I'm almost getting misty reading this, because I haven't read it in so long. Do you think he really listened to the demo? Reading this letter 19 years later makes me realize how lucky a 20-year-old kid was to get a letter like this. He gave me a real critique, which is what I wanted. It was fantastic and made me better.

From the moment I met him, I got a feeling of sincerity and knew that he was going to do our show and listen to my tape. I just didn't expect him to go to the length that he did. When you picture meeting a guy whom you've idolized, you worry about what he's really like when you finally meet him. Harry was so genuine. I grew up in the '80s listening to Harry Kalas and Richie Ashburn in South Jersey. I lived in Buffalo, New York, until 1981, and remember Harry from NFL Films. You always immediately identified that voice. Listening to him do games, I always felt like I was a part of it.

The biggest thing that meeting Harry showed me was that if I ever made it in the business, I want to be just like him and help the next guy. He meant a lot to me. He was an example of how to be a professional.

—**Ed Benkin**, KYW News Radio, Princeton Sports Radio

Chapter Two

PUT ME IN COACH

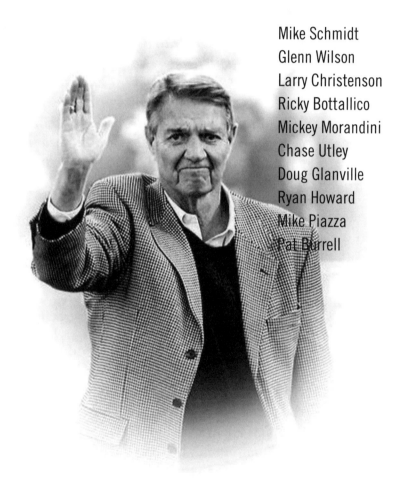

Mike Schmidt
Glenn Wilson
Larry Christenson
Ricky Bottallico
Mickey Morandini
Chase Utley
Doug Glanville
Ryan Howard
Mike Piazza
Pat Burrell

Playin' Favorites

M-I-C-H-A-E-L J-A-C-K

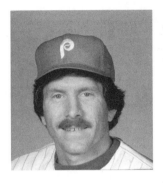

Mike Schmidt

Mike Schmidt was the greatest player in Phillies history, and a first-ballot Hall of Famer—yet in some ways he was immortalized by Harry Kalas' use of his middle name whenever he'd make a big call about the Phillies star third baseman: Michael Jack Schmidt. Kalas was Schmidt's biggest booster, and Schmidt has said that Kalas' constant on-air praise—Kalas regularly reminded listeners that Schmidt was the best player in baseball—often kept the fans at bay when Schmidt went through some of his notorious struggles.

A guy working in the booth describing the game to the fans has now established himself as even being bigger than the players that played the game. I'm a pretty big name over the years in Philadelphia sports history, as are a few of the other Phillies, and other teams had great players. I can't imagine a guy that could be bigger than Harry Kalas.

He's a household name. He's a guy they depended on for 40 years. I'm just a guy that played for 17 of them, just like all the other Phillies. We come and go. The guys that are here now, they're going to be gone. We're all going to move on. Harry was just always here. He was always here for you. If you can look past Ben Franklin and William Penn, he may have been the greatest person to grace Philadelphia in the history of the city, when you think about it, as many lives as he affected over the time that he lived in Philadelphia, who would have had a bigger impact on the city? Who would have? If anybody can think of somebody, I'm willing to hear it, but I don't know.

Schmidt was the only former player to speak at Kalas' memorial service, and he asked that his eulogy be included in this project:

Death brings unwanted emotions: fear, loneliness and finality. Death tests our faith. We can't hide from it. Its reality hits hard. Some will take longer than others to let it run its course. Our Harry Kalas is gone. We can't bring him back; we must grieve. But we also must not allow our grief to overpower our ability to celebrate his life.

Psalm 116, Verse 7: *Return to your rest, O my soul, for the Lord has dealt bountifully with you.*

I interpret that to mean God has called Harry home after a charmed and gifted life, a life in which we were fortunate to share. Is there any word that describes Harry Kalas' life better than bountiful?

There was nothing about Harry that suggested anything other than bountiful—the good times, smiles, fun, simply making people happy. Think about this man—millions of people from March to October, for 40 years, every day, depended on him for entertainment. Working people, construction workers, office workers, cab drivers, the elderly—hospitalized and homebound—even children. Everyone's lives were made better by Harry.

I've had hundreds of phone calls and e-mails from friends. Fans have placed flowers around the city and stadium to honor his life. One friend said he had listened to Harry over 4,000 times.

He and we players had a special relationship. Built on respect, we shared serious inside baseball discussions, but we also had our Harry sayings, facial expressions, and gestures, like a bunch of young kids. We loved when he made us look good, as he always did, during a game. Often he'd stop in the clubhouse before a game to take our temperature—to pump us up, as they say. It always seemed he knew what was going on with each of us. He'd reference a hot streak, a great play, someone's history against a pitcher, anything to lift our spirits and confidence. He did this for 40 years, with a natural sense of timing. Heck, he could even make me smile before a game.

Personally, I'll always have a reminder of Harry. Every day some-one refers to me as "Michael Jack." It's actually a brand. Over time, he branded all of us in some way. It was the same with every hitter and their home runs, every pitcher and their strike-outs, every employee, broadcast partner, and fan from every era. No one missed out. If we confronted him, or he us, it was always a special moment. It was never about him, always about us.

Harry left us too soon, and with that came a jolt. We weren't prepared. We never got to retire his mike, give him a retirement sendoff night, or build his statue. Funny, he presided over all of our special ceremonies, but never got his own. All we can do is ponder his existence. Reminisce about his life. Imitate his styl-ish delivery and recall his dry sense of humor. Most important, though, is Harry's legacy. A simple legacy, yet on God's list it ranks near the top. It's not the voice that will ring in our ears, the 40 years of dedication to his work, or his passion for the game. It's that every day he was inspired to make people happy. His smile, his tone, simply his way, affected us. He made us feel good, and that brought him a level of joy not many of us will ever know. It's a high calling of which few are gifted.

The Philadelphia Phillies are truly a family, and have lost a beloved member whose life should be celebrated. I believe God inspired Harry to take his unique gift of voice, and passion for baseball, and use them for good.

Harry carried that mission out, left nothing in the booth, and I believe was recently greeted at heaven's gate with, "Well done, my good and faithful servant."

Nothing more can be asked of a man's life.

Harry, thank you for entering all of our lives, and making them better, and our prayers are that God's love and grace will be with your family forever.

SOMETIMES GOD JUST HANDS YOU ONE

Glenn Wilson

Darren Daulton (L) dressed as Richie Ashburn and Glenn Wilson (R) dressed as Harry Kalas emcee the pre-game Harry Kalas Hall of Fame tribute at Veterans Stadium in August 2002.

Glenn Wilson was a major league outfielder for five teams from 1982–93. He played for the Phillies for four seasons, from 1984–87, and enjoyed his best year in 1985—driving in 102 runs, leading all National League outfielders in assists and making the All-Star team. He named his youngest son after Harry Kalas.

In 1984 in spring training I was traded from Detroit to Philadelphia with six days to go in the spring. I just drove over from Lakeland to Clearwater. Harry was the second person I met in the Phillies organization. It wasn't to do an interview. He just wanted to come over and introduce himself and say hello. I'd been traded a few times after that, and no one in the broadcast booth ever did that. You know, most people when they come to talk to you, they need an interview or something like that. Harry just took the time to come over and introduce himself.

I'd heard his voice from years past. I was a big **NOTRE DAME*** football fan and NFL football fan, so I knew his voice. And I was probably more excited to meet him than he was to meet me.

---

*The Oakland A's colors are green and gold because their late owner, Charles O. Finley, grew up in La Porte, Indiana and loved **NOTRE DAME** . . . when he bought the Kansas City A's, he changed their uniforms to the Notre Dame colors . . . The Green Bay Packers also adopted Notre Dame colors because Curly Lambeau played at Notre Dame.

I have a simple way of describing Harry: He's the greatest man I ever met. If you tried to pattern yourself, like Christ, he would be the pattern as far as how to treat humanity.

I was around him four years. I was with five teams in my career. And he was the only former teammate—and I'd call him a teammate—that I stayed in touch with every year. For me, because I lost my father when I was five years of age, I was constantly in search of a father figure. It was like that father figure was given to me when Harry came over to introduce himself. And it was immediate. I didn't know anything about the man, I just knew his career. His influence on me was so strong, and his friendship with me was so awesome that I ended up naming my youngest son after him.

His name is Andrew Kalas Wilson. I begged my wife to let me name him Kalas Wilson—thinking, man, what a tough cowboy name that would be—but she said, "No, everybody will think it's like a callous on your hand." Come on. Kalas Wilson. Classic. But we named him Andrew Kalas Wilson—and one day A.K. is going to be a great major league baseball nickname.

Harry wrote a note on August 9, 1991, after my son was born in July. He wrote it on a piece of Phillies stationery, and my wife had it framed. It hangs in Andy's room, right next to where he sleeps. It's on his bedroom wall. It says:

> I begged my wife to let me name him Kalas Wilson— thinking, man, what a tough cowboy name that would be—

"Welcome to the wonderful world of life. You have a beautiful mom and dad, a wonderful grandmom, and two great brothers, Glenn and Lance. Hundreds of years ago, a man named Shakespeare penned the words: 'This above all: to thine own self be true. And it must follow, as the night the day. Thou canst not then be false to any man.' Those words are true today as when they were written. And the wisdom of the words will always apply. When you are honest with yourself, Andrew, you are then able to give of yourself. And have human compassion for your fellow man and woman. Kane, Eileen and I are anxious to meet you. If there is ever anything that you need, and I am able, I will always be there for you. God bless and keep you well, Harry Kalas. I am both proud and humbled that my name will be a part of your legacy."

I get emotional every time I read it.

I look at my son, and I think about Harry. There's a constant reminder.

I sat with him more than any ballplayer in more hotel bars. And the most amazing thing was the fact that he never said anything negative. About anybody.

He was a teammate without ever putting on a uniform.

At Veterans Stadium, he would get into the booth right about the time my group was getting ready to hit in batting practice. So I would always throw a ball at him. He never complained about it. He had to dodge a few. I never hit him. But it became a ritual. It was going to take place. That was my love offering.

My 30th birthday was in 1989. I was with the Pirates. And my wife asked him if he'd fly in to emcee my birthday party. It was a surprise party, and sure enough he flew in and emceed my party. I'd been out of Philly since 1987. That's the kind of guy he was— "wouldn't miss it for the world, Willie."

Once I was sitting with him in San Francisco in the hotel bar and he was talking to the barmaid. We get up to leave at closing time, and he turns to me and says: "Willie, I'm going to marry that girl." I said, "Harry, that's called lust." "No, no, Willie," he said. "Something deep inside tells me that I'm going to marry that woman." I said, "OK, well, whatever you think. Good night." Well, the next thing I knew, he ended up marrying her. That was Eileen. He called it on the first night! I just said: "Harry, if you could start calling home runs before I come to bat . . ."

I thought it was hilarious at the time. But he knew. He loved her from the moment he met her.

After his divorce from Jasmine, who I loved and thought the world of, she wanted this condo he had in Clearwater. I was constantly teasing him: How's that condo situation? And he said, "That condo is history, Willie. Like a 3-2 pitch to Michael Jack—outta here."

Our relationship, in just four baseball seasons, was like this: Whether I was having my worst day, or my best day, I needed to share it with Harry.

I don't exactly feel like I've lost him. I feel like I gained so much from knowing him, that I could pick up the phone and call him. Whenever the Phillies would come to Houston, I'd see him. It was mandatory; it was like going to see my dad. I was always bragging about Harry, telling people that I knew him and showing him off when the Phillies would come to Houston. When his voice was on the TV, whether he was doing a game or doing a commercial, I always told people: "Sssssh. I'm trying to listen to Harry."

I can't think of any other broadcaster, for sure, or front-office person, who the team felt like that about. Harry was . . . well, he was the team. Even though he wasn't on that field with you, he was with you. Harry was one of the guys. Harry was not a writer that was off-limits, or someone who you wouldn't share everything with. Harry, you shared everything with him. Because you knew it was like putting it in the bank.

It was his humility. Harry was the most humble man. And in our eyes, as ballplayers, he shouldn't have been. He should have been the cockiest jerk that ever worked in the industry. He was an icon. He was bigger than Mike Schmidt, he was bigger than anybody in uniform. Harry showed that it was cool to be humble. In my day, you never thought about humility except when you were being interviewed. Then you'd be humble. But the rest of the time, there's pressure and stress, and you're not always so humble. Harry was the epitome of humanity. If he told you something, you could take it to the bank. He was total trust, he was total love. He was genuine.

Even in his faults, you couldn't condemn him for any of his faults, whether it was having one too many toddies or one too many ciggys. Or whatever. And the funniest line he ever told me—and I've stolen it, but I always wind up telling people where I got it— was we're on a flight, and I smoked, too, and still smoke, but I said to him: "Harry, don't you think you're smoking kind of a lot? Isn't that too many?" And he said, "Willie, I'd smoke 'em in my sleep if I could get someone to hold 'em for me." I just about fell out of my chair.

I'd always think: How did he do that? Not just bring me joy, peace and happiness, but also make me laugh like that.

When they clinched it, I heard Harry's call: *"Let the city celebrate."* What a great line to go out with. That was Harry's last World Series. It was almost like he knew. After you go through the mourning period, celebrate the legacy of something you're never going to have again. To see somebody capture a city the way he did, capture players the way he did, you're not going to see that again. The human brain cannot come up with enough nice words to say about this man.

> To see somebody capture a city the way he did, capture players the way he did, you're not going to see that again.

The honor was just getting to know him. Just getting to know the man—the man behind the mike.

TAKE THIS JOB AND LOVE IT

Larry Christenson

Larry Christenson, 55, pitched 11 years for the Phillies (1973-83), winning 19 games in 1977 and going 83-71 in all. Forced by injuries to give up baseball at age 30, he settled near Philadelphia, and has for the last 24 years run his own investment company.

In 1972 I was drafted No. 1 by the Phillies, and I came back to Philadelphia. I watched Steve Carlton throw a three-hit shutout against the Pittsburgh Pirates; that was during his 27-win season. I was just a high school draft choice from Everett, Washington, and brought some family members. We were watching from what was the family box at the time, and I was drawn into the broadcast booth with Harry Kalas and Richie Ashburn. They interviewed me: "You're the No. 1 draft choice. What do you expect?" That's when I first met Harry. He was blond and was wearing a colorful jacket. And Ashburn had a hat. I didn't even know who Richie Ashburn was, really. I'd never even really heard of the **PHILLIES***. I thought Phillies were horses, but I finally found out a few years later. So I was pretty naïve and young. But I remember meeting Harry Kalas, and that voice that he had. I found out a little more about him, that he was a newer announcer and that Richie Ashburn was a former player. Ironically, Ashburn and I became very good friends, and he actually bought my condo from me when I retired from the Phillies. My arm fell apart, and he bought my condo; I negotiated a good deal with him.

---

*The teams with the most losses in the four major sports: the **PHILLIES** (over 10,000 losses), the Warriors (NBA), Blackhawks (NHL), and Arizona Cardinals (NFL).

I built a good relationship with Harry Kalas, too. A lot of respect as just a friendly man that you wanted to be around, whenever you saw him coming. You couldn't pass this guy up. You couldn't pass up saying "hi" to him. I couldn't pass up getting his attention.

Remember, back in the '70s, there was no sports television, except mostly on Sundays. Then PRISM, a Philadelphia-based cable outlet, came along, and as I recall it was the first time that they started televising evening games . . . Harry Kalas would come down into our locker room before the games, and even sometimes after the

> I'd never even really heard of the Phillies. I thought Phillies were horses . . .

games. He always wore these colorful clothes. He always had colorful slacks and a colorful sportcoat, open-collared shirt and had his blond hair, and had his white belt and white shoes. You hardly ever saw him with anything other than that.

When I was growing up as a young player, he was always very friendly on-air. He was always very friendly pregame, postgame, traveling on the bus, traveling on the plane . . .I had a lot of different nicknames, but mostly it was Chris. I really didn't like that. I didn't use it, or I didn't say it. Then a player came along and shortened my name; it was L. C. Just L. C. Shortened it up. Harry's the one that ran with it. Harry's the one that announced it on the air. To this day, the reason I'm nicknamed L. C. is because of Harry Kalas. Nobody called me L. C. ever until Harry used it on the air. That was when my nickname took.

Harry was always having a good time. Just a friendly, friendly man. Just friendly, everywhere we went. He had me pegged as L. C. I had him pegged as Harry the K. And so in greetings, I'd go, "Harry the K!" He'd go, "L. C.!"—you know, in that deep voice. At other times we'd be sitting together, riding along, or I'd come and sit down next to him on a bus getting to the airport, or on a plane. And he goes, "L. C.—he winds and here's the pitch: He struck him out." Or he goes, "There's a long drive . . ." He would have fun with his announcing and his voice, as a friend, just relating to you. He'd go, "Michael Jack Schmidt—that's outta here." That was his way to even say hi to Mike Schmidt. Or, "**PETER EDWARD ROSE***." Or, "Lefty" to Steve Carlton. And he'd usually give it a "swing and a miss." So it wasn't like, "Hey Harry, how ya doin'?" It just wasn't like that. It was like a normal, "Hey, what's up?" It was always a long greeting and a handshake and a hug, and an appreciation for each other, and friendship. Nobody can take away his love for baseball, and his love for what he did.

The fun times were on the golf course with Harry and Whitey. What Harry would say when he made a putt was, "ka-lunk-a." Our greetings later on would go, "Harry the K—ka-lunk-a." Then he'd go, "L. C.—ka-lunk-a." So that was our later greeting. Then one of his favorites was, he would sing a little song when he was walking down to the airport gate . . . He had all these little things he did. But boy, I'll tell you—if there was a piano bar somewhere, that's what really made him happy, because if he wanted to have a drink and a cigarette and just sing, and just interact with other people, he was so happy in that atmosphere. That was his release, and where he was happiest. He just had a lot of fun.

He would sing anything—ballads, **SINATRA***. But he would always mix in a "High Hopes." That was the last song of the night. Or when he felt the time was right and he could get the piano player to engage in that, he would do that at the opportune moment. He sang "High Hopes" more when he was asked. He'd sing "High

*PETE ROSE** is enshrined in the Summit County (Ohio) Boxing Hall of Fame.

*When Bobby Thomson hit "The Shot Heard Around the World" in 1951, Frank Sinatra and Jackie Gleason were at the game. When Thomson homered off Ralph Branca, Dodger fan Gleason did a technicolor yawn (vomited) on Sinatra's shoes . . . In the late '60s during an Old-Timers day at Shea Stadium, Thomson hit a Ralph Branca pitch into the left field bullpen . . . In the movie *The Godfather*, Sonny Corleone died while listening to that game . . . Dave Winfield was born that day.

Hopes" because that was another legacy he left. Rather than him doing it on his own, he was always coaxed into it, urged: "Harry, please sing 'High Hopes.'"

As far as the team goes, we loved it when Harry entered and walked through that locker room. If he didn't even say anything—there were so many guys to say hi to—if he just walked through and waved, that's all we needed. We got a little bit of Harry that day, and it put a smile on our faces. On mine, especially. I feel I can speak for Tug McGraw, the late relief pitcher. I was just talking to Lefty the other night, and we just laughed. When we think of Harry, we've just got to giggle, because he was just a No. 1 fun guy.

He had his watch set on East Coast time, and whenever we traveled anywhere there was a time change, he never, ever changed his watch. If you'd asked him what time it was wherever the team had traveled, he would always say what time it was in Philadelphia.

He also kept everything from years past in his wallet. He had a wallet that was, like, four inches thick, with business cards. You'd give him a card, and he'd put it in his wallet. He never removed it. We'd say, "Harry, let me see your wallet." And he'd pull this wallet out and hold it up, and it looked like a big, old, triple cheeseburger.

We accused Harry of taking "No Ass At All" tablets, because he had no butt at all. So he put that wallet in there, and it pumped out the one side out a little bit. We said, "Well, it's good, because at least it gives you one side of a rear end."

I did hear him announce, plenty of times. As a starting pitcher, Carlton and I, a lot of times, instead of sitting on the bench all the time, we'd take a little break and walk up to the locker room. Lefty was watching a lot of the game on TV, listening to Harry and Whitey and everybody else. But I got to hear Harry quite a bit, hear him announce and hear him on the radio, especially when I was retired. I retired at a young age, and I've been in Philadelphia for a long time. So I heard Harry for many, many years announce. And he's just a wonderful person to listen to, with that voice, and he's just right on, all the time . . . That microphone was just magic with him. It was just magic. I mean, how many times did you ever hear him stutter, or make a mistake? It just didn't happen.

It was 1980, the Mount St. Helens blast. I had elbow surgery. I was in Washington State, rehabbing and healing up from surgery. I was doing my exercises and trying to get back in shape—which I did. I came back and pitched later that year. But Mount St. Helens' first blast was in May of 1980. The second blast went off in June of 1980. My grandmother and friends collected the volcanic ash from the first blast. They collected volcanic ash, which was all over the ground in the whole state of Washington and other states and Canada. But they picked up this real soft, fluffy, brown ash from the first blast. Then the second one was almost like a gray sand from the beach. And so, what happened was, it was Richie Ashburn and **TIM MCCARVER***, who was brand new in the booth. Because remember, McCarver had played on the field with us briefly that year, to get four decades in. But he was new to announcing.

I brought McCarver some ash from each one of these blasts, and he was telling Richie Ashburn about it. Certainly Harry Kalas is listening to all of this going on. What happened is that Richie got one of his little jabs in. Timmy said, "Well, you've got this one ash from this blast, and this one, and they're different." And Richie Ashburn said on the air, "Well, Timmy, I guess if you've seen one piece of ash, you've seen them all." McCarver's jaw dropped, and he thought right there he's out the door—no more job, he's going to be fired. Whitey just laughs it off, and he carries on, and tries to draw McCarver back into the broadcast. Certainly, to Harry Kalas, that was one of the funniest things he's ever heard on a television or radio broadcast. We always talked about that,

---

*Brent Musburger was the home plate umpire when **TIM MCCARVER** made his pro baseball debut for Keokuk, Iowa, in the Midwest League in 1959.

because McCarver stayed on another couple years or so, and Richie and Harry always brought that up, about McCarver and the ash story. Just to hear Harry laugh about it—every time, it would bring a big bundle of laughs from him.

One of the all-time remembrances of Harry Kalas was when I was in St. Louis. It was 1981, the strike year. We had started the season; we opened up in St. Louis, and we all went out the night before the workout—not before the first game, but before the workout, which was on a Thursday; the first game was on a Friday. Carlton was pitching the first game, and I was pitching the second game. And I was in great shape.

We all went out to this place call Muddy Waters, which was in the Gaslight District, near the Mississippi River. We were having a good time, listening to the comedians. I got lured out into the street by this kid. I went out into the street to see what he wanted . . . Boston Bruins star Phil Esposito a few months prior had gotten lured out and gotten sucker-punched by a rugby player. Well, I got sucker-punched by a rugby player, too. They knew we were athletes and they got me; I was the one that went out, and I turned around after I just shooed the kid off and a big old knuckle-burger sandwich came and just smoked me, and shattered my nose. I didn't go down. I got hit really hard. I didn't lose my balance. I scoped him out and ran after him, and all heck broke loose. My teammates come running out of the bar and restaurant, going every which way. McCarver went one way, chasing someone down the street. Del Unser got tackled into the gutter, and his feet were going up and down. I was trying to break the guy's arm on a pole, the guy that punched me, because he was hiding behind a car.

Harry was in there. I don't think Harry came out into the street, but when it was all said and done, here I am, bleeding like crazy, and I've got to walk back to the hotel. We've got to walk underneath the Arch. Who's there with me but Harry. I'm all bloody. I've got a rag under my nose, and all I recall is that he's trying to give me advice on the fact that these things just shouldn't happen. I said, "Harry, it's over with. I got sucker-punched, and my nose is broken." He said, "What are we going to do, L. C.? We've got to get you back to the hotel." He's got a cigarette, and I think he carried a drink out of the bar . . . So he walked me back with a cigarette in his mouth, giving me a bit of a talk: "L. C., I'm so sorry that this happened. It just should have never happened." I don't recall everything that was said. All I remember is that Harry walked me back to the hotel and made sure I was OK. It was a moonlit night. We're walking under the Arch, and Harry's talking about, "Look at this wonder of the world." And here I've got a broken nose. I really couldn't have cared less about the Arch.

I had to go to the hospital. They said my nose was not broken. A few months later I went to the doctor, and he said, "My gosh, this thing has been shattered, and it healed the wrong way." That was one of my strolls with Harry—with a broken nose, under the Arch in St. Louis.

The Hall of Fame induction, I would never miss that. I went up in '94 with Carlton, '95 with Ashburn, '96 with **JIM BUNNING*** and then 2002 with Harry. So we were up there, and Harry was going around, and he was so proud and happy, greeting everybody.

I like to remember him as when I played, or the years that I followed and watched. But I just knew that he was having a rough road healthwise in recent years. He fought through it and didn't complain. Now he's gone. We all miss him. We miss him terribly.

*When **JIM BUNNING**—now a U.S. Senator from Kentucky—retired from baseball in 1971, he had more strikeouts than any pitcher in history other than Walter Johnson.

CULTURAL LEARNINGS OF THE BULLPEN FOR MAKE BENEFIT GLORIOUS KALAS NATION

Ricky Bottallico

Ricky Bottallico was an all-star closer for the Phillies and pitched 12 seasons in the major leagues. In addition to having one of Harry Kalas' favorite names to say, Bottallico used to joke about the idea that Kalas was awarded the privilege of sitting with the players on the team plane—Bottallico always said he thought it was the players who got to sit with Harry on the team plane. He now works as a radio and television analyst on pre- and postgame Phillies broadcasts.

The first time I met Harry was actually when we came up to the Vet for the young-timers game. He came up and introduced himself, and just hearing him say my name: "Rick-y Bo-ttalico!" I grew up listening to him do **NOTRE DAME*** football and hearing Harry Kalas say things like, "Touchdown, Allen Pinkett." So when I heard him say my name, I just thought: "Wow, that's awesome." Those are the things you remember, the way he said your name.

I remember sitting with Harry and Whitey on the team plane, and we'd play blackjack. Whitey would deal and say, "Read 'em

---

*The "**NOTRE DAME** Victory March" has won multiple polls as the greatest college fight song ever. It was written in 1908 by two alums, John and Mike Shea. John Shea, who wrote the words, lettered in baseball at Notre Dame before taking his volley cheer on high in 1965 in Holyoke, Massachusetts. . . . . In the late '60s, almost one-third of all junior high and high schools in the United States used some version of the "Notre Dame Victory March" as their school song.

and weep, boys." Harry's big thing was to double the dozen. Any time he had a 12, he would double his bet. He wouldn't always double 11, like you're supposed to, but if he had 12 he would double it every time. And Whitey would say, "Oh, geez, Harry, you got me again!" Those two together were unbelievable.

> He always had a positive spin on things.

I used to sit with him on the plane. And when I'd sit down next to him, if I'd had a bad game, he'd say, "What was that, a hanging breaking ball?" And I'd say, "Yeah. Things are rough right now." And he'd always say, "Don't worry about a thing, Ricky B. You'll be out of it in no time." He always had a positive spin on things. And then he'd hand me a **COORS*** Light and say, "Here's your backup slider."

One of my favorite Harry stories was after 9/11. Harry was really distraught about 9/11. We all were. When we came back, it was really emotional night for the players, for the fans, everybody. We went up to the press club after the game, and there were a bunch of people up there. Harry was in the middle of this huge mix of people—players, clubhouse people, media. We were having a good year that year, and we had a shot at the division. We were playing the Braves, and it turned into a "badmouth the Braves" edition up there, everybody was going nuts on the Braves. It was fun. And then Harry broke out with "High Hopes"—and then "God Bless America." It was awesome. If I could have bottled it, I'd live that night every night with him. It was special. That kind of night, that's not something that happens all the time.

I was the closer, so I'd sit in the clubhouse early in the game and watch the game on TV. So I heard him a lot. The only time I ever heard him call anything I did was on the highlights or replays. The most memorable one was right before the 1996 All-Star

---

*In the upper deck at **COORS** Field in Denver, there is a row of seats that is painted purple all the way around the stadium to signify the mile-high altitude level.

game, when I gave up a three-spot to the Expos. I had two outs, and Cliff Floyd hit a home run off me. Harry knew I was pretty much a lock to go to the all-star game if I didn't fall apart. And it was the Sunday before the picks came out. And right before the ball got hit, his call was: "There's the 2-2 to Floyd . . . I DON'T BELIEVE IT!" That call stuck with me because it was so heartfelt, more than anything. He wasn't saying: *Ah, he gave it up.* He was saying: *Oh, I feel bad for him.* That was Harry's personality.

Harry's personality was heartfelt in everything he did. And it came across on radio, or TV, or when you were talking with him. And that's why people loved him.

MIC-KEY
MORE . . . . AND DEAN . . . . EE

Mickey Morandini

Mickey Morandini played second base for the Phillies from 1990–97, and made a return engagement in the final year of his career, playing 91 games with the Phillies in 2000. In 1992 he turned baseball's first unassisted triple play since 1968, getting three outs on a line drive against the Pirates on Sept. 20. He was also quite possibly Harry Kalas' favorite name to say.

It's a great feeling being the name everyone loves to say. Everytime I come to Philadelphia or Florida for a fantasy camp, or even sometimes in Chicago, where I was with the Cubs in 1998–99, a lot of fans come up to me and say my name like Harry. It's very flattering. Sixty or 70 percent of the time, people have to say my name like that, and it's almost as if there's no other way.

I've known Harry a long time and we became good friends. Legendary Cubs broadcaster Harry Caray in Chicago could never say my name right, so that was always a big joke too. He would say a lot of different things—Morandino, Marinaro; he seemed to say it differently every time. As for Harry Kalas, his unique pronunciation didn't evolve, either; I always remember it sounding like that. I don't remember it being different, especially when good things happened. When I hit a home run, scored a run or made a diving play, that's when he enunciated my name. It's really a great honor.

Before Harry, they just said it like it's written, and quickly. Morandini. Pretty boring, actually. Harry brought it to life by putting the emphasis on the syllables and it took off from there. I never said my name like that, but it surprises me how many people do. Every time I meet somebody, they always say it like Harry used to. A lot of people normally have trouble saying it, so maybe Harry helped people pronounce it.

I grew up in **PITTSBURGH*** listening to Bob Prince, Milo Hamilton and Lanny Frattare. I didn't really listen to Harry until I started playing with the Phillies. When I think about Harry Kalas, the Phillies, NFL Films and Campbell's Soup pop into my head. Those are the things you remember right away. You always knew right away whose voice it was.

> Harry Caray in Chicago could never say my name right, so that was always a big joke too.

I'll never forget the night we sang "High Hopes" after clinching the NL East in 1993 in Pittsburgh. We're in the training room icing down with some cocktails and celebrating when all of a sudden Harry starts singing. The glow in the players' eyes, and the respect for him, was obvious. It was a magical moment for him to be singing in the training room and everybody joining in. That's how much everyone loved him. The respect came from how he broadcasted. He did the game, told it like it is. He didn't rip players. He saw it like it was, and players respected that. He never said anything behind your back.

My favorite moment was singing "High Hopes," but the favorite call was probably Mitch Williams striking out Bill Pecota, and we were going to the World Series. That was a combination of winning the National League, Harry calling it, and the excitement. When Harry spoke, people always listened. He was very unique and everything he said came from the heart.

To see the Phillies win the World Series in 2008, months before he passed away, you couldn't have asked for a better ending. I know I will always miss hearing that voice and seeing the man.

*There was never a no-hitter at **PITTSBURGH**'s Forbes Field . . . but it was the site of Babe Ruth's last home run . . . as a Boston Brave in 1935.

I'M THE MAN

Chase Utley

The Phillies All-Star second base-man quickly became a fan favorite due to a hard-nosed style that works well in rationally blue-collar Phil-adelphia. Utley is known for an unmatched intensity on the field and a tireless work ethic. He's also known for not smiling in games despite being surrounded by more ebullient sorts such as Ryan Howard and Jimmy Rollins. Make no mistake about it, Utley loves the game and loves his surroundings and quickly became one of Harry Kalas' favorite players.

[It's August 9th, 2006, and Utley is standing in the sun on a hot Wednesday afternoon, taking in the moment at second base in Atlanta's Turner Field. Utley had just hit a one-out, three-run double to give the Phillies a 4-2 lead. This has happened before and will certainly happen again, but what came next defined the player Utley was and is, with six simple words from Harry Kalas.

Ryan Howard pulled a high chopper that Braves first baseman Scott Thorman fielded and touched first to get the second out of the inning. In most cases, the runner at second would have stopped at third, but Utley isn't most players and instead, he never slowed as he rounded third base and scored under the tag of former Phillies catcher Todd Pratt. What Utley didn't know then was that high above the field, Kalas was at the play-by-play microphone coining a term that is now a part of Utley's life.

"Chase Utley, you are the man!"]

Once he said that, everyone was saying it. Obviously, I didn't hear him make the call, I was on the field and we were in Atlanta. But after the game, several people told me about it, and it felt like everyone started saying it. They were saying it on the field and in the clubhouse, but it really dawned on me what had happened when we got home. Everyone in the stands started saying it, and then it was on signs, so everywhere I went I heard it or saw it.

It speaks more of the man and the respect people had for Harry than it does about me. Once he said something, I don't know, it became fact. If Harry said something, it was written in stone and there was nothing anyone could do to change that. I guess I should be glad he said that about me.

Look, he had a trademark. He trademarked a lot of nicknames and a lot of sayings and whenever you hear one of them, you know it's Harry Kalas. I know after that day he said that phrase a lot, and I'm happy to be associated with him in that way.

Harry was special, there is no doubt about that. He was in here every day and he would go get his coffee and then say make his rounds. It was part of his routine, but it was part of our routine as well.

> "Chase Utley, you are the man!"

I don't know if this is a good story or not, but as you know and everyone around here knows, I'm pretty focused prior to the games. And every once in a while, he'd come in 20 minutes or 30 minutes before the game, which is usually my "stay away from me" time, maybe even an hour or so, OK, but really, 30 minutes before a game—stay away.

But he was Harry, and every so often he'd come in and say, "Chase, could you come outside and talk to these kids? They are really big fans of yours."

Anyone else . . . I just couldn't say no to Harry. I could never say no. He did it three or four times and I could never say no, just because of the respect I had for him.

IF A PICTURE IS WORTH A THOUSAND WORDS, A WORD FROM HARRY IS WORTH A THOUSAND PICTURES

Doug Glanville

Doug Glanville played six seasons with the Phillies, including the best year of his career in 1999, when he batted .325 with 204 hits and an NL-leading 149 singles. It's also possible Glanville led the majors in IQ during his career, having majored in systems engineering at the University of Pennsylvania. Among his many business ventures following retirement in 2005, Glanville serves as a guest columnist for The New York Times, *where he wrote a Harry Kalas column after Harry passed away.*

I appreciated Harry so much. Growing up in the '70s and 80s'watching games of the week, you had timeless voices, like Vin Scully's and Joe Garagiola's. The way they said things brought the game to life. As a player from my generation, part of the excitement of making it was having legends of the game call your name. Going to **YANKEE STADIUM*** and hearing Bob Sheppard say, "Now batting . . ." was a big, huge part of your big-league arrival.

Whenever we flew into a city, he'd be in the lobby with his signature white jacket and white shoes. He just always had time for players. It was constant. He'd lend his golden voice to the team's fantasy football draft or anything. Bobby Abreu basically called him, "Struck him out." Every time he saw him, "Struck him out."

---

*Thomas Edison sold the concrete to the Yankees that was used to build **YANKEE STADIUM**. Edison owned the huge Portland Cement Company. . . . Edison's middle name was Alva, named after the father of onetime Cleveland Indians owner, Alva Bradley.

I became a Phillies fan as a kid in Teaneck, New Jersey, because I thought they had the coolest uniforms. I loved infielder Dave Cash. That's how it started, but it really grew from there, and Harry was a big reason why.

I got my first career hit at Veterans Stadium off Terry Mulholland on June 10, 1996, and my only career inside-the-park home run on May 10, 2002, versus Arizona. I knew as I rounded the bases that the moment was being immortalized by Harry's description—even if I couldn't hear it live. Players could go entire careers without experiencing Harry's calling their great moments, and that is a great loss for them. I knew that my home run story was being told so that anyone listening would not only understand what was happening, but feel every spike hit the turf as I rounded second.

> I became a Phillies fan as a kid . . . because I thought they had the coolest uniforms.

Pretty quickly after I got back to the dugout, I thought about how Harry would describe it. I listened to it within hours of it happening, and that made it more exciting. That was always the beauty of it. He brings it to life for everyone, not just myself. There are always emotions you can't express when you're actually doing it, but they're there because you were once a kid, too. He did a tremendous job of translating the moment. People always felt what he felt. He took that responsibility of being that conduit to the viewers to the highest level.

Harry was the people's voice, connecting everyone to everything in a game he loved. He gave meaning to events. He didn't just provide a walk-through of a great play; he embodied a convergence of perspective and emotion and approached it all as if it was his duty to share every morsel of it. There was no emotion left on the table with Harry Kalas—you heard, you felt, you understood everything that was happening.

If Harry didn't describe a play, it was almost as if it never happened.

THE MAN WITH THE GRAPHITE ARMS

Ryan Howard

Few Phillies players have been able to steal the national spotlight in the manner Ryan Howard has since he joined the Phillies full-time in 2005. The "Big Fella" as Harry Kalas called him was just that from his first day on the roster en route to the 2005 Rookie of the Year Award and 2006 Most Valuable Player Award. Howard's ability to hit home runs (he reached 100 career home runs faster than anyone else in history) and to hit them great lengths were center stage at the 2006 All-Star Game in Pittsburgh, where he immediately became one of the most feared power hitters in the game.

There weren't too many times you could say no to Harry because he was the type of person that exuded happiness and class. He cared about everyone and always went out of his way to be nice. He was the genuine article and it's impossible to explain what he meant to this town.

I guess I was lucky that I grew up in St. Louis. Growing up we had Jack Buck, so I could understand how people could grow to love an announcer and feel as if they were a part of the family. What Jack Buck is to St. Louis, that's what Harry Kalas is to Philadelphia.

> What Jack Buck is to St. Louis, that's what Harry Kalas is to Philadelphia.

There were no boundaries for Harry because of who he was. Ten or 15 minutes before a ballgame, he'd come up to you and ask you for a favor—an autograph or if you could stop by for a second and meet some fans. It wasn't that you couldn't say no; it was you didn't want to say no. You knew that Harry was doing this only because he wanted to see everyone happy and enjoying baseball. Why would we say no to Harry when we knew darn well that if the tables were turned and we asked him to do something for us, there's no doubt in my mind he'd do it for me or for anyone on this team or in this organization.

The first time I met him he came up to me, said hello and wished me good luck. I had an idea who he was and looking back, again, it's comparable to me meeting Jack Buck. At that time, I really didn't have the grasp for the magnitude of what he stood for. Again, I'm sure everyone has said this, but that voice. It's the guy from NFL Films or those Chunky Soup commercials. That's pretty cool. All of that stuff came to mind because HK was all of that too.

You know what? The first time I heard "High Hopes," I thought, wow, that's interesting. But the more you hear it, the more you get used to it. I like all kinds of music, so the more I hear it, I have to admit the next thing you know you're singing along with it. I don't think I've ever heard it as much as when I got here and that's all because of HK. You also have to understand, the more we won, the more we were going to hear it. Every celebration over the past two years has included HK singing "High Hopes," so it's more than just a song.

> Every celebration over the past two years has included HK singing "High Hopes," so it's more than just a song.

I would definitely say for us, one thing that we can look back on is winning the World Series while he was still with us. I had heard he didn't get to call the World Series in 1980, so yeah, we did something special for him last year, but we did something special for everyone in this city and in this clubhouse. Being on the verge in 1980 and Harry not being allowed to call it for the national guys, and then being so close in 1993, with us doing that last year—for him to be able to call a World Series—was something special.

PIAZZA'S HOME RUNS WERE REALLY JUST EXTRA BASE TRIPLES

Mike Piazza

Mike Piazza is arguably the greatest-hitting catcher in major league history, finishing his career with 427 home runs and 1,335 RBIs and 12 all-star appearances. He also grew up in Norristown, and attended Phillies games as a kid. In the 1996 All-Star game in Philadelphia, Piazza had a double, a homer, two RBIs and was named the game's MVP. He is the only player Harry Kalas announced as a Little Leaguer and as a major leaguer.

The voice is the first thing that stands out when I think about Harry and the distinct cadence. It's so recognizable. He was a huge part of my youth and an inspiration to me. He made me want to be a baseball player.

There were many nights with my dad and brothers, when we'd go to a game, but have to leave early because we had school the next day. The Phillies would come back and win. Honestly, it was a blessing that we left early because we'd be in the car and got to hear Harry. When Harry said something, it was always an extra-special experience. One game Del Unser had a pinch-hit home run to win. We were in the car, and suddenly you would hear, "Swing and a long drive . . ." You knew something great had happened. It was great for me to hear that.

You can make an argument now that with so much coverage today, it's not the same. You don't get that hometown feel, the identification with the city. In this age of so much media coverage, with highlights and more highlights, and the ability to watch games on the computer, it seems like people don't listen to the game. They get the highlights. It's different when you hear nine innings of a game and listen to it unfold. Listening to games with Harry and Whitey meant more to me than anything. If you were a baseball fan driving through Philadelphia, Harry was all you had, and you were lucky. Now you can watch any game you want. It's not a bad thing, per se, but it's different.

When I was 11, I played on a Little League All-Star team, and one of Harry's sons, Brad, played, too. Brad's team was playing against us and Harry came to the game. Everyone went nuts, saying, "Harry Kalas is here!" Then Harry went up to the booth and announced a couple of the player's names. Wow. I remember my friend saying, "I didn't have anything for him to sign, so he signed my sneaker." So my friend has a signed sneaker from Harry Kalas. I don't even think I was playing in that game, but it was so cool that he came. That made him larger than life for me. Luckily, he announced my name later.

I even remember going to a Phillies game in the seventies and Harry caught a foul ball. I remember watching him catch it and everyone cheering. I always looked for him whenever I went to a game. Then there were the days at the shore as a kid in Wildwood, New Jersey. We'd sit and listen to the games, and we would get the Mets, Yankees and Phillies, so I would get Phil Rizzuto, Bill White, **BOB MURPHY***, Ralph Kiner, as well as Harry. I really had a tremendous childhood in that regard, and a lot of it was with Harry. The random calls always were my favorite. I always liked, "Here's the pitch: Swing, big cut, no contact" or "Here's the 2-2 . . . Swing and a chopper down the line . . . [Tim] Wallach barehand throw—not in time."

I'll never forget my first homer against the Phillies in Los Angeles, off Jose DeLeon. Somebody game me a tape of Harry calling the

---

***BOB MURPHY** was the Voice of the New York Mets for 40 years. His brother, Jack, was a sportswriter in San Diego. The latter was so influential in bringing major league baseball to San Diego in 1969 that the city named the park for him: Jack Murphy Stadium.

home run the next day because they knew I'd want it. I remember the call: "Swing and long drive, deep right field, outta here, home run Mike Piazza. The rookie Piazza shows some good opposite-field power." Even though it was against the Phillies, he still had a nice call. That was a big rush. I played it over and over again in my car.

You always knew that Harry wanted the Phillies to win, and it probably broke his heart to call my home runs. I hadn't really thought about it like that until now, but I'll take what I can get. One time I had a good game against the Phillies. I hit a home run off Mike Williams, and he gave it a good call: "Home run to center field." I have tapes of a lot of his calls. Once I hit a walk-off, and I think he just said, "Oh, brother." That was funny.

I remember listening to games and where I was when I heard certain moments, and I remember specifically thinking that I wanted Harry to call one of my home runs. He called a few of them, even if he didn't enjoy calling them. The Phillies were the team I rooted for growing up. They were my team. When you're a kid there's always that dream of playing for the team you're rooting for. It would have been fun to play for the Phillies, and it would have been great to have Harry get excited about one of my home runs.

But like I said, I'll take what I can get. It was always fun for me to come back to Philadelphia and especially to do well at the Vet.

In 1993, Mike Piazza's father, Vincent, and his partner in a computer company wanted to invest $27 million of the $115 million needed to move the Giants to Tampa Bay. The move was blocked by MLB. The two sued to overturn baseball's antitrust exemption. MLB paid Piazza and his partner $6 million in settlement.

LIFE, LIBERTY AND THE HAPPINESS OF PURSUIT

Pat Burrell

Pat Burrell came to the Phillies with high expectations not only of himself but of a fan base that believed the No. 1 overall pick out of the University of Miami in 1998 would change the Phillies franchise in a positive manner. Burrell's selection came one year after J.D. Drew refused to sign with the franchise and left a bad taste in the mouths of Phila-delphians. Burrell had a very close relationship with Harry Kalas, who enjoyed the fact that Burrell, now the designated hitter for Tampa Bay, was called "Bait" by his teammates during his rookie campaign. So much so that he used it as code in his scorebook whenever Burrell advanced a runner and even when he inter-viewed Burrell after games on television.

It all just seemed to happen so fast. It was as if I had just seen him. It was a week or two earlier that I saw him at the World Series ring ceremony. The next thing you know, H wasn't with us anymore. After all that happened that day, seeing him at the ceremony, giving him a hug, it just seemed fast.

It's funny, a lot of people bring up that he flew in the back of the plane. The truth is, that's where he smoked. Before, when you could smoke on a plane, it was back there. That's where you could be so that's where he went. He'd be back there with Larry Andersen and a couple of other people. I had never seen any-thing else. It was all I knew and I thought that's just where he belonged on flights.

The biggest thing of all, to me as a person, not a ballplayer, was he was always very kind to me and my family. He went super,

super out of his way to be nice to my folks and that's something very special. Not everyone does that and no one that I've known has done it like H did.

The other thing is he treated everyone the same. He was so genuine that you couldn't turn him down. Every year, I knew there would be one night I didn't have my suite. Every year, H would come up to me and say, that his doctor buddy, Mazz (Bob Mazzley) needed the suite and every year my answer was the same, "Yeah H, you got it." You don't turn Harry down because you respected him so much and you knew whatever he was doing was coming from his heart and genuine.

You know what's amazing about the nickname "Bait." Todd Kalas has the scorebook from his games. I didn't know until Todd showed it to me, but every time I advanced a runner, he'd write "bait" along the base path. I have a copy of it and it's hysterical. I don't want to make H look bad so I don't know if this should be in the book but then, the joke isn't really on him, is it. My wife Michelle knows and that was long before I started dating her. I guess it's fine, then. This all started because of Larry. It started with this inscription of "Bait" on my glove. This is because of the Mizuno guy. LA undercut me and had them put it on the glove.

But he always called me "baitage." So in the scorebook, he'd write "bait." When I saw Todd had a copy of it, I had to laugh. Todd said, "I don't know if anyone is going understand this." But I do, which, is great. You know, he said it on the air numerous times. It was hilarious.

I saved a voice mail that Harry sent me when I signed with Tampa. It's unbelievable. For him to call for one, you don't expect anyone to call because it is what it is. He left me a message, so nice and so thoughtful and it was almost like he was sad. It's just so sad he's gone.

Quick Hits and Interesting Bits

When you are in the minor leagues, and by that I mean the Phillies minor league system, the goal is to hear that voice say your name. If Harry Kalas says your name, then that means you've made it to the highest level of baseball.

For me, I guess that took on added significance since it took me so long to get here and what I went through to reach the Phillies. Not even a home run call, although when I heard that for the first time I got a chill. I just wanted to hear him say my name because then I had finally made it.

In 2006, when I almost made the team out of spring training, we were getting on the plane to fly back to Philly. Now, I had never met him. In spring training, you didn't see him as much; he didn't come into the clubhouse as much, and it's just different from the regular season when you see him every day and he says hi to all of us every day.

Anyway, as we were getting on the plane, I see him and he says, "Hey, Chris," in that Harry Kalas voice. He said, "You're having a great spring. Keep it up. What a great story. Just keep it up."

I was blown away. He knew about my story and what I had gone through and had paid close enough attention to say something to me that made me feel really good. It was an honor that he even knew who I was.

Look, I was still just a minor leaguer. Yeah, my story had gotten a little more play and plenty had been made about me on the verge of finally making it into the major leagues, but the fact he knew who I was blew me away.

I talked a little about it in my book. We did those exhibition games before the season, and one of the highlights was he did the introductions of the team before the games. To hear him say my name over the P.A. or anything was amazing.

—**Chris Coste**, Phillies catcher and author of the book
The 33-Year-Old Rookie

It's the voice you can't forget. He's always been in the back of my mind, as far back as when I was playing Wiffle Ball in the backyard, introducing Pete Rose, Mike Schmidt, Larry Bowa and Manny Trillo. It's the voice I deeply cherish. It's amazing that one person's voice can bring so much happiness to so many people. He's touched so many people who grew up with him.

I remember being a kid in 1980. As soon as you turned on the TV, you couldn't wait to hear that voice. I always tried to imitate him. In my mind it was pretty good, but it can't be duplicated. Getting to the big leagues was a dream come true, but it was so much more special when that voice said your name.

We first came to Philadelphia when I played for the Cardinals, and I couldn't wait to meet Harry because I was excited to meet the guy who was my idol growing up. It was 10 times better once I met the man. I put him on a pedestal, and once I met him, he was on a higher pedestal. My wife, Julie, is not the biggest baseball fan. We were in a packed elevator at the Vet after a game when Mr. Kalas gets on. He starts talking and my wife says, "I know that voice. That's Mr. Kalas." She grew up with that voice, listening to games with her grandfather. She's not really a baseball fan but immediately recognized the voice. It brought back many memories of her childhood, and that's what Harry does.

I always referred to him as Mr. Kalas because I respected him so much. He would always say, "Call me Harry," and I'd say, "No, it's Mr. Kalas." I would always tell him what a pleasure it is to listen to him and how many fond Phillies baseball memories he gave me throughout my childhood. What made him so special was that he cared about every situation. If he got emotional, you got emotional. If he laughed, you laughed. It could be the sixth inning of an August 5 game and it would seem like it was the first pitch of the World Series. Harry always brought that out. I'll always remember how excited I was to hear Harry call Mike Schmidt's 500th home run. That was unbelievable to hear that.

I was fortunate to have had the unique experience of growing up a fan, then getting to hear him announce my name. I hit my only home run in Philadelphia during the last year of Veterans Stadium on July 21, 2003. As I'm rounding the bases, it was like 30 some-odd years of memories going around in one swing. I thought about how Harry called this and every memory of my childhood flashed in front of me. I enjoyed that home run more because I had never homered in Philly and I knew they were going to knock down Veterans Stadium, so I pictured every day of Wiffle Ball, Legion Ball, Little League, high school, college . . . It was 30 years of memories wrapped up in one trot. I still have the ball. It's way up there on my list of highlights.

—**Joe McEwing**, former major leaguer from Bristol, PA

 Harry and I had a pretty good relationship. We lived in the same neighborhood in suburban Philadelphia. A lot of times coming back from road trips, I'd give him a ride home. And we'd talk about the road trip— the good things and the bad things. The one thing I respected about Harry is that on those trips, I probably said a little bit too much out of frustration, maybe—things that probably the general public shouldn't be hearing. And Harry was always very, very professional and never repeated the things that probably shouldn't be repeated. I respected him very much for that.

He was a very, very smart baseball man. If he wasn't as much on the broadcast side or would have played the game, he probably would have ended up as a manager, and probably a darn good one.

He loved life. He lived it to its fullest. The world is definitely lesser without him.

—**Von Hayes**, former Phillies outfielder, manager of the Lancaster (PA) Barnstormers, in the independent Atlantic League

He was a class guy. When I would go in there as a visiting player, he was always very accommodating to me because I was a Pennsylvania boy from East Petersburg, some 90 minutes west of Philadelphia. He also seemed to go out of his way to talk to me. He always treated the average players the same way he treated the superstar players. He was just a real fair, easily accessible guy.

The friendship thing became a part of it when I played for the Phillies. The announcers are there every day with you; they're in the clubhouse. I spent a lot of years in St. Louis with Jack Buck. They almost become a part of the team. You do have a different regard for them, because they're always there.

—**Tom Herr**, former infielder and current bench coach
for the Lancaster (PA) Barnstormers

To me, the one thing that really stands out to me was he was never negative. Let's be honest, in Philadelphia there can be a lot of negativity from announcers to media and so on. That's just the way it is and you come to accept that but with Harry, he was never negative. He was always positive. I grew up in Southern California, so to me, the play-by-play man was Vin Scully. Harry shared a lot of qualities with Vin Scully and one of those was his optimism. That didn't come across just because of his voice, although I'm sure that had something to do with it. It's just that he always allowed the game to play out and always believed the best would happen.

The one thing that will always stick out to me, that I'll always remember, is that when I signed with the Dodgers, he was one of the few people that called me. That's just a little thing and something you don't even think about. It's not necessary or something you expect. It's the way of things. In this game you move around and you move on. I was a little different in that I spent all those years with the Phillies, but everyone still understands the nature of the business. But Harry called me. It was just ten seconds but that small gesture meant a lot.

I heard "High Hopes" at least six times a year, sometimes more. Yeah, it's not a song I heard a lot growing up. It tends to grow on you. At first, you never know what to think but it doesn't take long, maybe a couple of minutes, for you to enjoy it and understand that this song is Harry. You know all the words and you enjoy every one of them when Harry sings them.

—**Mike Lieberthal**, Phillies catcher (1994-2006)

 Early on he knew a lot about Hawaii and I asked myself, "How does he know so much about Hawaii?" I found out later that his first wife was from Hawaii and that he spent the early part of his career broadcasting games in Hawaii. That was interesting to me, especially since he knew so much. One day I hit a walk-off home run and he said "Shane Victorino, No Ko Oi," which means "number one" in Hawaiian. That's what Maui is known for: "Maui is No.1." Only he would know it.

I suggested two tributes for Harry that we did. First, before a game against the Nationals we took a cigarette and each took a brief smoke from it. Second, Mrs. Kalas gave us Harry's light blue jacket and white shoes to put in the dugout each game.

The two tributes were and are definitely obvious things to do in my mind. He was a part of this team and he knew everything and everyone from this team. He was a part of the family and we knew him as well. A lot of teams, when something like this happens, will hang a jersey. I just asked Frank Coppenbarger, what do we always see Harry in—that jacket and those white shoes. It's an honor and it's a grand gesture for his wife to give us those items. That shows both what he meant to us and what we meant to him. I'm sure it wasn't easy for her to do, but that makes it even more special to us.

It's just one of those things. He's always going to be missed. You think of him every day because he was with us every day and now, something is obviously missing.

—**Shane Victorino**, one of three current Hawaiians
on major league rosters

 It was always the subtle things that aren't amazingly interesting that define Harry. The Clark Griswold shoes are the best things ever. The blue blazer and the white shoes are the HK staple. That's the image I'll always remember. We'd be getting on the bus and he's outside the bus smoking a butt, white shoes, blue blazer . . . seeing that was always an amazing, comfortable feeling.

When I was drafted in 1997, I came to the Vet, and they took me to the press box. I was up there watching the game, and met Harry Kalas. Growing up in L.A., you know the voice more than the name. I remember he said, "Nice to meet you" and I'm like, "Oh my God, it's the NFL Films guy!" I had no idea what he looked like, and it was so weird hearing that deep voice in person. When I got called up in 1999, it was awesome getting to know him. I always felt a friendship. HK was untouchable, and the level of respect for him was indescribable.

Chipper Jones always killed us, a lot of times. We'd be up 5-3 and he would hit one. Harry would say, "'There's a long drive to left and [lowering his voice] that's going be all." It was almost like he said, "Ah, crap." He's calling the game objectively, but you know what team he wants to win. There's the White Sox guys, the extreme—4-0 good guys—but HK would say good things about the other guys. I loved the "fastball down the middle for a ball," little things he was as impartial as you could be, but you could tell he was rooting for the Phillies and really wanted them to win.

—**Randy Wolf**, Phillies left-handed starter 1999-2006

Chapter Three

IT WAS A BALL

Larry Shenk
Pat Hughes
Howard Deneroff
Frank Coppenbarger
Larry Costigan
Bill Giles

Extra Innings
with Baseball People

WORKIN' FOR THE PHILLIES WAS LIKE PLAYIN' HOOKY FROM LIFE

Larry Shenk

Larry Shenk joined the Phillies in 1963, working as the team's public relations director. Nicknamed "The Friendly Baron," Shenk was there when the Phillies first hired Harry Kalas and helped coordinate the caravans—a winter barnstorming tour for the Phillies that continues to this day—that not only promoted the Phillies but initially introduced Kalas as the team's new voice.

The first time I saw Harry was 1965, and I didn't know who he was. He was broadcasting with the Astros. I was sitting in the third-base dugout at Connie Mack Stadium with Gene Mauch, and Harry comes walking across the field. Gene says, "What is this guy's name?" I said, "I don't know. I didn't know who he is, or what he does. I've only seen him sitting at the far end of the pressbox." I later learned that was because he was only doing one inning a game on the radio. That's the first time I saw him—but I didn't know who he was, or what he was doing. And then he came here in 1971.

I don't remember making the press announcement. But it was not a popular move. I don't recall specifically how bad the initial reaction to Harry was. But it was probably minimal. We didn't have talk radio, we didn't have Comcast doing 6,000 shows, we didn't have the Internet. It was basically print. But it was not a very popular move. It was more about Bill Campbell, who was very popular, than it was about Harry. Still—the way Harry treated people? It was just a matter of time.

It was part of our changing our image—when Bill Giles came,

we changed our uniforms, we changed a lot of things about the team, we started to do more promotions in the media. And Harry was our emcee for all of it. Harry was the emcee for our dedication at Veterans Stadium when we played our first game. And we didn't realize it at the time, but he forgot to introduce Chub Feeney, the National League president, who was on the field.

Vince Nauss tells the story, once we stopped at a fast-food place and everyone is ordering: I'd like a cheeseburger, whatever. And then you'd hear this voice: I'D LIKE A CHEESEBURGER AND FRENCH FRIES AND A VANIIIIIILLA MILKSHAKE. That voice, it was just beautiful the way he could make anything sound.

He was always our emcee. I was always not in charge of that stuff, but just organizing the sequence, who would follow who. But I'd never write for him, I'd never have to write anything about Juan Samuel; I'd just tell him: Juan Samuel. And Harry would do it. Why would I put words in Harry's mouth? He was great to work with that way.

It was really odd that for so many years we were having tributes and he was The Voice. And then on April 18, he was the subject. That's when it got me.

I never saw him angry. I don't think he ever said a bad word about people.

And, you know—two blond-haired kids from the Midwest captured Philadelphia. Ashburn and Kalas.

Whitey was such a classic guy. He'd tell these stories, and Harry would crack up. Harry had his cigars and his cigarettes, and Whitey had the pipe. It was tough for Harry when we got here to Citizens Bank Park because there's no smoking in the ballpark.

I mean, Whitey would tell these stories—like when a player breaks or loses his favorite bat, how difficult it is, and Harry would ask something like whether players would take their bats from the ballpark back to the hotel for safekeeping—and Whitey would say, "Yeah, I took a lot of old bats back to the hotel in my day." Whitey had that dry sense of humor. There's the story Harry always told, how Whitey would mention Celebre's pizza and they'd send him pizza during the game. Finally the Phillies told him to stop it; they weren't sponsors, stop giving them free advertising. But we could still do birthday wishes, so Whitey would just say, "Happy birthday to the Celebre twins—plain and pepperoni."

It just clicked. I don't think you'll ever see anybody like that again.

> Did he ever really recover from Whitey? I don't know.

When Whitey died . . . Harry was amazingly strong. His eulogy was awesome.

Did he ever really recover from Whitey? I don't know. There might be a trickle of truth to that. Whitey certainly had an effect on Harry.

We all remember Whitey. We all told Whitey stories. We still do. I don't remember Harry ever saying: "Boy, I really miss that guy." He said it in a different way. That's the way he'd always talk about him, tell those Whitey stories. That's how he kept Whitey with him.

None of it was ever rehearsed. "This game's easy, Harry." "Bet your house on this one." It just came out. "Hard to believe, Harry." They just keep coming back.

Look, I'm an old person. But today there's too much talking on television. It's just talk, talk, talk all the time. Too many experts talking all the time. But with them it was just a relaxing conversation. It was just your two uncles, talking baseball in your living room. And you were there.

At the end, people said Harry struggled as a broadcaster. But still, when he'd make a big call—goosebumps.

When we were on the road, we'd go to the hotel bar after the game and Harry would always be there. He loved to talk baseball and argue. I used to tease him about Mike Schmidt—and I really liked Mike Schmidt—but I knew how much Harry loved him, so I'd say, "Ah, Schmidty strikes out too much." And Harry would say, "WHAT DO YOU MEAN, HE STRIKES OUT TOO MUCH?" And off we'd go.

I don't remember the exact circumstances, but one time coming back from the caravan Harry had something to do the next day—early. So he decided to stay at the Holiday Inn here near the ballpark instead of going home. So he stays out late, and when he goes past the front desk, Harry said to the lady working there, "Will you kindly give me a wake-up call at 6:30?" She says OK. He said, "My watch stopped. What time is it?" And she said, "It's 6:15." Yeah, that would happen once in a while.

He'd emcee every banquet. He did the sportswriters' banquet, all of them. He loved doing those things. He just stepped up and did it. He loved to tell Whitey stories. He was just so good to people.

His relationship with Chris Wheeler got so strained. But when Wheels was my assistant here, they were together all the time. I mean, it was nauseating the way they acted with each other. I'm sitting here, working my butt off, and they're partying and carrying on.

And yes, it got strained. But at the end, Wheels protected Harry in the booth. And they got better as time went on.

The last few years, we'd send Harry to a senior citizens' place and he'd sing Christmas carols. Just this last December, we were set up for 11 a.m. on a Monday. And Harry winds up doing a Sunday night football game in Indianapolis. So Rob Brooks, Phillies director of broadcasting, told Harry not to worry about it. Harry said, "I'll be there." And he got a 6:30 morning flight out of Indianapolis, just so he could be there to sing Christmas carols to the senior citizens.

He didn't want to take time off. Harry was at a point where he could have done what he wanted to do. He could have done just Monday and Wednesday home games, whatever he wanted to do. He didn't have to travel. But he didn't want to retire. He used to say, "I can't retire. What'll I do?" I'd tell him, "Harry, you've got the voice. You can do voice-over work for the rest of your life." But he couldn't retire. He didn't want to give it up.

At the Hall of Fame weekend, we had a lot of people there, we had the family there, we had a tent and we had a big party for Harry. And it was really cool. He was great. Whitey griped about it when he went in. We had to go to a press conference when he'd been inducted, and Ashburn said, "I just may not go to Cooperstown. What do you think about that?" I said, "You'll be robbing your family of the greatest day of their lives." And he said, "Welllllll . . . we'll see." Now, that was not Harry. Harry could not have been more thrilled.

After Whitey was in the Hall of Fame, he said one time, "This Hall of Fame stuff sucks. You don't have any more privacy any more. Everywhere you go, people are bothering you." Harry never felt that way. He treated everybody great; it didn't matter who you were—an intern in the hallway he didn't even know or the president of the United States, he treated everybody the same.

> "... I don't want to be the first person to say, 'That's one ball on John Kruk.'"

The inductees have a pretty rigid sched-ule. We were out of town, and it was hard for Harry to get away and come to the Phillies party. But he did it, and he showed up and he sang "High Hopes"— and it was just awesome.

He was treated like a player. The fans held him up on the same level. And the players all loved him. He could talk to them like nobody else could. When John Kruk came back from his surgery for testicular cancer, Harry went up to him before his first game and said: "John, do me one favor—swing at the first pitch. I don't want to be the first person to say, 'That's one ball on John Kruk.'"

It wasn't just his sense of humor. Harry had a way of saying things.

He was not a prima donna, like some people can get. He was a great human being.

When Whitey died, we won 1-0. His uniform number was 1. When Harry died, we won by one run—9-8. The last time Harry and Whitey worked together was 9/8 (Sept. 8). Harry's favorite player was Mickey Vernon, who played for the Washington Senators. Harry died in Washington. The day of the tribute here, they were naming a Little League field after Mickey Vernon. Harry was going to go. I was going to go.

People say it isn't the same. Well, it's not the same. It can't be the same. Christine Negley, the Phillies' manager of publications, spent so much time and did an awesome amount of work on the magazine we put out after Harry died. She combed through all the files of photographs for hours. I said, "Christine, you're really doing a lot of work on this." Her answer was, "Anything for Harry."

A lot of guys, Joe Buck, Al Michaels, the Carays, they did national broadcasts, too. But I don't think it fit for Harry to be broadcasting the **REDS*** and the Cubs someday. I'm sure he had opportunities. But he belonged here. He was ours.

We were blessed to have lived with the man for all those years. We really were. It was too short. But we were blessed. No doubt about it.

*In 1998 the Cincinnati **REDS** started an outfield trio of Chris Stynes, Dimitri Young, and Mike Frank. You might know them better as Young, Frank, and Stynes. (The author couldn't resist. He'll show himself to the principal's office now.)

MANY PEOPLE ARE CUB FANS BECAUSE THEY CAN'T AFFORD WORLD SERIES TICKETS

Pat Hughes

Pat Hughes is in his 13th season as the WGN Radio play-by-play voice of the Cubs. He joined WGN in 1996 after spending the previous 12 years teaming with Bob Uecker on the Milwaukee Brewers Radio Network. He worked in Minnesota in 1983 as the TV voice of the Twins and as the hockey host/interviewer on North Stars telecasts. Hughes was named the Illinois Sportscaster of the Year in 2006, 1996 and 1999. Hughes is a graduate of San Jose State University.

I did a commemorative audio tribute to Harry Kalas on my baseball voices series in 2007, called "Harry Kalas, the Voice of the Phillies." It is on www.baseballvoices.com. My series contains six CDs and Harry is one of the six. On it, I talked about the fact that he has a great voice. But he combined that natural gift with a superior work ethic. That's really what made Harry the special broadcaster he was. He could have easily just coasted through his career and earned a good living on the basis of his voice alone . . . but, that was not Harry. He loved baseball. He loved performing. He loved doing the voice-overs for NFL Films.

When I told Harry I'd love to do a CD on him, I gave him my Harry Caray and Jack Buck CDs. He said, "These are really beautiful." About two months later, I asked him if he had listened to them, and he said, "Well . . . I really don't have one of those CD players." When I finished producing his CD, I had to dub it over to a cassette and send that to him. He and his family listened to it with his wife, Eileen. Not only did he call back with great graciousness and respect and friendship, he said, "My wife and I listened to it. Thank you so much. In fact, my wife wants to thank you." And he puts her on the phone. That's the first time that had ever happened to me. He couldn't have been nicer.

He did not have a mean bone in his body. It was great when he would call me at home and leave a voice mail. I wouldn't erase it for months just so I could hear his voice. Last December I was promoting the CD on one of the Philadelphia radio stations. I had a lot of good things to say about Harry, and I'm trying to sell the product. Well, he happened to be listening at the time. He called that night and left a beautiful phone voice mail message for me. He said, "You know, Pat, I was going to NFL Films and was listening to the show, and there you were and you start talking about me, and thank you so much." It was so great to get a voice mail from Harry Kalas. I felt like I was a 10-year-old kid again . . . and I saved it.

I first met Harry when I went to the National League in 1996. He was kind and was always friendly. He always had time for me. He was never too busy doing preparation or anything. He always would stop what he was doing and would look you in the eye. He would talk to you. There was something very calm and very kind about Harry Kalas. He had no discernible ego, even though it would have been completely natural for him to have a gigantic-sized ego. He was a unique talent in that he probably could have worked in the so-called "major" markets of New York or L.A. or Chicago . . . but he loved Philadelphia. He stayed there, and he had no intention of ever leaving.

He would get there early—always three hours before a game—and would go right to work. He's got his highlighter pen and is writing down notes. If you listen to the games, it was obvious that he knew what he was talking about.

Baseballvoices.com is a website full of highlights, humor and history. Harry Caray and Jack Buck were the first two I did. Marty Brennaman was number three. Then Harry Kalas and Bob Uecker were simultaneously released. I just came out this spring with Red Barber. I am doing these CDs on the guys who have inspired me, educated me, entertained me—people I feel like I really admired . . . people I enjoyed listening to . . . and people I learned from. I loved listening to his voice. It's a magical sound. The voice-overs he did for NFL Films were classic. When I played the CD for my wife, I put on his voice in one of the very first tracks. My wife heard his voice, and she said, "Jeez, honey, I thought *you* had a good voice." Obviously, Harry had one of the greatest voices ever.

On his CD, there's a track called "Michael Jack Schmidt Early," where Harry calls his 500th home run—great radio call. I have the story of "young Harry" growing up.

Harry is from Naperville, Illinois, a suburban Chicago town. He went to a White Sox game around 1945. It was a rain delay. He was sitting down near the Washington Senators dugout. Mickey Vernon, who, I believe, that year would become the American League batting champion looked up behind the dugout and saw this cute, 10-year-old, blond-headed kid—Harry Kalas. He said, "Hey, kid. How you doing?" Harry said, "I'm okay." Well, Mickey said, "Come on down, kid, and sit in the dugout with us." He lifted Harry Kalas up so he could go into the dugout with him. He gave him a baseball, autographs it . . . has the other guys on the Senators' team autograph it. He treats Harry like a king. From that day on, Harry said, he fell in love with baseball. Also, he became a life-long Washington Senators fan. Mickey Vernon was actually in the audience the day Harry Kalas was inducted into the Hall of Fame.

I have a rare piece of tape that Harry Kalas did not even know existed. I call it "the Astrodome opener." It was the first-ever exhibition game at the **ASTRODOME***. In those days, Harry was doing one inning only of play-by-play. He's working with Gene

*On June 15, 1978, the Pirates were "rained in" at the Houston **ASTRO-DOME**. Ten inches of rain flooded the Astrodome parking lots and access roads. The teams made it to the park, but the umpires, fans, and stadium personnel did not.

Elston and another man. Harry is doing one inning . . . and I couldn't believe it when I hear his inning—the first words he says are "Mickey Mantle, Bobby Richardson and Roger Maris coming up for the Yankees." I was stunned. I put the whole half inning on. It was a one-two-three inning. It's great listening to Harry talk about Mantle and where he is on the all-time home run list, and Richardson and Maris. It's great . . . and he loved that. By the way, Mantle hit the first-ever Astrodome home run that day.

I have on CD the time when Willie Mays scores from first base on a routine single to left field. He was not running on the pitch . . . and there was no error on the play. You have to hear Harry describe it. It's classic. It's a great base-running play told by a great baseball announcer. It's complete history. That's track seven.

I talk about Harry going to Philadelphia. Bill Giles was instrumental in bringing him there. I've got Harry calling some plays from a Cubs-Phillies game—the final score 23-22. I've got some great calls of Harry Kalas from 1980 when the Phillies won it all. He made some magnificent calls. Mike Schmidt and Bake McBride hit home runs. I personally think that's Harry's greatest call. It's late in the season. Bake McBride beats Montreal 2-1 with a ninth-inning solo home run at the Vet. It's Harry Kalas at his absolute best. I have some National League Championship Series. That series in 1980, Houston and the Phillies, four games went extra innings. It's a best of five, and four games went extra innings! It's unbelievable. The Phillies are down in game five 5-2, on the road, in the eighth inning, against Nolan Ryan . . . and the Phillies win the game. It's just great. Harry is on television, working with Tim McCarver. McCarver had played for the Phillies earlier in that year. He was injured and that was the start of his broadcast career.

Track 12, for Cubs fans, is sickening. Harry Kalas is working for CBS Radio in 1984 calling the so-called "Garvey game."

In 1980, there was a network exclusive contract where local announcers could not broadcast World Series games. CBS radio did them. Here's Harry—his whole life he wants to broadcast a World

Series. His beloved Phillies make it . . . and he's left outside . . . left out in the cold. It was awful. But, it's a great story, as Harry tells it on the CD. He says that Philadelphia fans were so outraged and so disappointed that they couldn't hear Harry and Richie Ashburn that they bombarded network executives and Major League offices. They flooded them with phone calls and telegrams. The very next year, they reversed the rule and allowed local announcers to be able to broadcast. It was because Philadelphia fans were so upset that they couldn't hear Harry and Richie.

I have segments of 1983 and 1993. Harry said that 1993 was his favorite team—the Lenny Dykstra and Darren Daulton and John Kruk bunch. He loved that team. They upset the Braves in the NLCS.

He's got a wonderful Richie Ashburn track, track 14. I'm sure you've heard the "going to bed with a lot of old bats" story. Harry is working on the air with Richie early in their careers. Harry says, "Richie, I'll bet a baseball bat is pretty important to a ball player." Richie says, "Harry, it really is. When I'm on the road, I never used to leave the bat in the clubhouse. I would take it back to the hotel with me . . . in fact, sometimes, I would sleep with it. In fact, I've been to bed with a lot of old bats in my day."

The whole CD is over one hour. I tell people I'm going to rewrite the CD to make it more appropriate, and I'm going to create a new legacy CD and I'm going to add some highlights from last fall where Harry did get a chance to broadcast a World Series championship. I will certainly add some of those.

I take the same attitude into every single park. You want to do it as well as you can. You want to try to have some fun. Be prepared—be ready for anything. Where I am is becoming less and less important over the years. To me, every single game, you try to reach a certain level. I've always liked Philly, but, to me, it's the same as going to the park in New York or Pittsburgh. It's that same eastern seaboard, very hot in the summer, very passionate fans, very fast-paced life . . . so I enjoy it. It won't be the same going into Philly without the smilin' face of Harry Kalas.

THE DOs AND DON'Ts OF WORKING WITH HARRY KALAS: DO!

Howard Deneroff

Even though he was raised in Queens, New York, as a Mets fan, Howard Deneroff chose to listen to Jack Buck during the 1986 World Series, instead of the Mets broadcast. Deneroff is a Coordinating Producer with Westwood One/CBS Radio Sports.

I went to school at Syracuse with Harry's son, Todd, so I've known Harry Kalas for a long time. Todd Kalas and I worked together a little bit at the school radio station. He was two years ahead of me.

Remember Syracuse is a broadcasting school so there is a lot of great talent there. Just as an example, Dave Pasch, your Arizona Cardinal announcer, is a Syracuse guy. Mike Tirico is a Syracuse guy. Ian Eagle is a Syracuse guy. Dave Ryan, who works for ESPN and does a bunch of stuff for them, is a Syracuse guy. There was a ton of good talent there when I was there. It's hard to say Todd was the best but because of what his dad did, he had a leg up and a better understanding of what was necessary for a broadcast. He was far ahead of the curve when we all got there because of him growing up in a broadcast booth. So . . . am I surprised that he's been in baseball as long as he has . . . no, he grew up around it and had that advantage that the rest of us could only dream of. Don't get me wrong—I'm not saying he got it because of his dad, because he didn't. You just pick up things by osmosis that none of the rest of us had been exposed to until we got to college. He had that his whole life.

I would have to say that he doesn't sound like his father—nobody sounds like his father. Harry had a one-of-a-kind, unmistakable voice . . . and, he was a one-of-a-kind unmistakable guy. He was different from any other announcer I ever worked with. He was just "one of the guys." That's not to say that other announcers don't fit in—that's not what I mean by it. The players will tell you that. Everyone in Philly will tell you that. He was just one of the regular guys who happened to have unbelievable pipes and was great at broadcasting.

I worked with Harry toward the later stages of his career, and I found him to be just like everybody's uncle. If you have a family member, there's always issues with your parents, and there's always issues with your siblings, but everybody loves their uncle. I don't know anyone who has ever had a bad word to say about Harry or who didn't love Harry.

You deal with people every day of your life, even the best people, somebody doesn't like them. Somebody will have something negative, "Oh, he's great, but . . ." There was no "but" with Harry. There really wasn't.

When it came time for our contract negotiations it was simple. He wanted to do the games. We wanted him to do the games. It was one conversation—boom—"send it to me, I'll sign it." I'd be foolish to sit there and try to negotiate with that guy. That's crazy. He's the voice of the NFL. What, am I not going to have him on my broadcast? Like everything with him, it was simple.

One of the first games I ever worked with Harry was on the road at Buffalo. It's a Bills game on a Sunday. Saturday we get into the Marriott. I asked him if he wanted to get together over dinner and go over material for tomorrow. He said he wanted to watch the big SEC college football game that day, so he suggested we go to a sports bar where the game would be on in the background while we talked. We go to a sports bar and there was about a 15-minute wait for a table. The hostess asked us if we would like to wait at the bar. We said, "Sure, we'll do that." We go over to the bar. It's crowded, but we can inch between some people to get to the bar to get the bartender's attention. Keep in mind, above the bar, there are about 16 televisions, but only one of them has sound—the college football game. As we sidle up to the bar, they flash the score of the game and then go to a commercial. A Coors Light commercial comes on. The bartender says, "What'll you have?" Harry says, "I'll have a Coors Light, please." As he's saying it, coming from behind him on the television is Harry's voice on the Coors Light commercial. The bartender says, "Excuse me." "I'll have a Coors Light, please." He looks at Harry—wide-eyed. He looks behind him. He hears that same voice coming from the television. He looks back at Harry and he looks back at the television, and he's freaking out. Harry said, "What'll it take to get a Coors Light here?" He points at himself. He points at the TV. He goes, "Yeah, that's me . . . and I think that would make it faster for me to get a Coors Light." He wasn't nasty about it or anything . . . it was just one of those moments. The guy was so flustered and said, "Sure," and looks at me and says, "That's really him?" I said, "Yeah, that's him." He said, "Oh, I can't wait to tell everybody." He didn't charge us for the Coors Light, by the way.

> He looks at Harry— wide-eyed. He looks behind him. He hears that same voice coming from the television.

It was just one of those moments in time. What are the odds of that happening in anybody's life? The bartender couldn't have been more than 22-23 years old. That's one of my favorite stories because of the look and the moment. Harry would have never said anything, but the guy had put two and two together because that voice is unmistakable . . .

Harry was great to work with, and he was terrific on a broadcast. He was the voice of NFL Films and did work on HBO. As I said to him a couple of years ago, when he asked, "Are you sure you want me back?" I said, "Harry, that's your seat. You tell me when you don't want to come back."

Look at the guys from Jack Buck to Ernie Harwell to Vin to Chuck Thompson to Bob Murphy—almost every Major League team has one of those guys. Almost every team—not everyone, obviously, the newer ones don't. Almost every team has "a guy." Oakland had Bill King. Jerry Coleman in San Diego. Herb Carneal in Minnesota. I'm not necessarily saying all those guys are in Harry's caliber or class, but . . . almost every team has a guy who has been there for 20 years, minimum. Now, we've lost a bunch of those guys—we've lost Harry, we've lost Herb Carneal, we've lost Jack Buck . . . Harry Caray. Seattle has Dave Niehaus. Toronto had Tom Cheek for their first 30 years of existence. Baseball is the perfect game for radio—there's that romance and that "sound of summer."

Football is a little different. There are couple of reasons for that. It's fewer games so there isn't as much attachment. You still have your Merrill Reeses in Philly. And Frank Herzog, who was there for 30 years in Washington. When he got blown out, you can't even imagine the uproar. It's tough to replace those kinds of guys.

There has also been a change of affiliated stations a lot more. You don't have the KMOX with a 50-year relationship with St. Louis Cardinals fans. With the changeover there's more tendency to change announcers. Right or wrong. And, in some cases, it may be a right situation.

Harry had an agent . . . and I spoke to him once, only because a client wanted Harry to voice their commercial. Our negotiations were always easy. We want you back. I want to come back. Let's do it. We had a one-page contract, by the way, which is pretty rare.

I'm different from most of the fans who listen on the radio. I adore all these broadcasters because I wanted to be them. They had my dream job, so I listened differently than most fans. I revered all those guys. When I first started here, doing baseball, I got to meet players . . . and I'm not going to say I wasn't thrilled at meeting the players . . . but it was a much bigger thrill for me to meet Harry and to meet Jack Buck and to meet Brent Musburger and whoever else crossed my path—Hank Greenwald, Mel Allen, Bob Sheppard—to me, much cooler. I used to walk around with a book, Curt Smith's *Voices of the Game*. I had every announcer I ever worked with sign it. I wouldn't let them sign it unless I worked with them. I've got a ton of autographs in that book—only announcers.

For football, the announcers have to do a spotting chart. For baseball, you have to do a lineup—a lineup card, a scorecard. I've never seen two announcers have the same version. No two announcers in baseball keep score the same way. If you took the way Harry Kalas scored a game, and you gave his scorecard to **ERNIE HARWELL***, and vice versa, I guarantee they wouldn't be able to recreate the game by reading the scorecard. Nobody would know what they did to each other's card. The only two people I've ever seen with the

> I grew up loving baseball and listening to these guys and I wanted to be these guys.

same scorecard are Bob Uecker and Pat Hughes when they worked together for the Brewers before Pat went on to Chicago. They shared a scorecard. Shared it. Both can look at it and know exactly what happened. But that's unheard of. No two guys keep score the same way—nobody. It's the same with football—they have to do a spotting board and nobody does that the same way at all, even though it's a basic template.

I don't root for teams. I root for PR directors. The better the PR director, the easier my job is.

---

*As a young man in Georgia, **ERNIE HARWELL** was Margaret Mitchell's paperboy. Mitchell wrote *Gone with the Wind* . . . Harwell was baptized in the Jordan River and later wrote songs that were recorded by Willie Nelson and Waylon Jennings.

THERE'S NO EXPIRATION DATE ON FUN

Frank Coppenbarger

Frank Coppenbarger is the Phillies' director of team travel and clubhouse services. Coppenbarger not only runs the Phillies clubhouse—a Herculean job in itself—he charters the planes, books the hotels, and is responsible for the Phillies' travel on the road. He joined the Phillies in 1989, after working in St. Louis with the Cardinals. Coppenbarger is the keeper of Harry Kalas' blue sportcoat and white shoes, which the Phillies have in the dugout during the 2009 season as a tribute. When the team isn't playing, the sportcoat hangs in Coppenbarger's office.

I'm very fortunate that I was with Harry for 20 years. Before that I was in St. Louis with Jack Buck for eight years. Two of the all-time greats. I'm pretty proud of that. When they had the memorial service for the ballpark, someone said they'd only done that for three people in baseball history. One was Babe Ruth. The others were broadcasters—one was Harry Kalas, and the other was Jack Buck. I worked with both of them. That's something.

In Chicago we stayed at the Hyatt on the Chicago River, a hotel that had two towers in it. One year Ronald Reagan was president, and we were staying at the hotel at the same time. So they put us all in one tower, whereas they'd usually separate the players and the staff in different towers when we had a night game at **WRIGLEY FIELD**.* So the president is in Chicago and there is all this hoopla, and we're trying to just get back and forth and play the

*More NFL GAMES have been played in the Meadowlands than any other stadium. Until 2003, **WRIGLEY FIELD** held the record even though Wrigley had not hosted an NFL game since 1971.

game. We're at Wrigley Field and we see these two big military helicopters flying toward the airport. It was a really impressive sight, although I didn't think much of it at the time.

That place had a hotel bar called "The Big Bar"—it was 200 feet long. It was the biggest bar I'd ever seen in my whole life. Well, Harry is holding court there, as he'd often do. My wife Christine was with me. This naval officer comes in the bar, in full dress uniform—he's got on the hat, the gloves, the jacket, the pants. All white, head to toe. He looks terrific. Harry loved guys in the military, so he immediately goes to say hello to him, and he brings him over and within 10 minutes he's part of our group.

Now, this bar is on the mezzanine of the hotel, and you could look down on the lobby below. There was a huge fountain down there in the lobby.

Harry starts singing. The night starts to get late. Harry is singing college fight songs. He's roped this guy. I remember his name was Ken, and poor Ken is trying to keep up. It's getting later and later, and we're carrying on, and finally in Ken's honor Harry gets us all singing "Anchors Aweigh." By now, whether any of us can actually sing or not, we're all great singers. And it's a great night.

By the end of it, Ken's hat wound up in that fountain. I wound up with his gloves; I had them in my pocket at Wrigley Field the next day. Poor Ken has his shirttail out, he looked a mess. And I remember thinking that Ken did not leave the bar looking as neat and perfect as he'd entered it. That was not an uncommon occurrence if you were hanging around Harry at that time.

We didn't think anything of it, but it turned out that Ken was part of the president's honor guard. That's why he was there. I just hope there wasn't too great a punishment for losing part of your uniform in a hotel bar with Harry Kalas.

I used to love to watch people's reaction when they got on an elevator with him. If they didn't recognize him, their heads would pick up as soon as Harry said something. When Harry would get off the elevator, as soon as the doors shut, they'd all say, "That's

Harry!" Or if we were in another part of the country, it would be, "That's the NFL guy!" or "That's the Campbell's Soup guy!"

No matter where we were, we'd be on the road on the other side of the country, and a commercial would come on TV and there would be Harry's voice. There was always the voice.

One moment that always sticks with me was in Wrigley Field, the first time Harry stepped in to sing "Take Me Out to the Ballgame" in place of Harry Caray. He sang great, and he did the whole act, swinging his arm like Harry Caray used to. All our players came out of the dugout in unison and tipped their caps to him. That showed you the respect they all had for him. That was pretty neat.

In 1993, we clinched the division in Pittsburgh after being so bad for so long. We were in that little clubhouse in Three Rivers Stadium. You know how you can have a party in your house, and you have this big, beautiful living room—but everybody winds up in the kitchen? That was

> I've never seen anything like the way the players felt about Harry.

Pittsburgh. There was barely enough room in the clubhouse, but at least it was a clubhouse—and yet everybody packed into the trainer's room, because that's where Harry was.

There wasn't enough room for 10 people in that trainer's room, but all the guys were in there with Harry. He really loved that '93 team. He was really part of the group. That team, they were rough to deal with at times. But he couldn't say a bad word about them. He was one of them; he was one of the boys. Of all the guys I've been around, I've never seen anything like the way the players felt about Harry. He was like a player.

To keep Harry's sportcoat and shoes with us was the players' idea—and I thought it was a really nice idea. At first I think the family found it a little odd. But Phillies team president David Montgomery told them that if this had been a player or a coach or a manager, we'd have kept their uniform up. Well, this was Harry's uniform. That really is Harry.

I'm avid Illinois fan, which everyone knows. If Illinois got beat, he'd let me know about it. If Illinois won, he'd sing a few bars of "We Are Loyal to You, Illinois." He was great like that.

Harry was so nice to my family all those years. If my kids were at the ballpark and the camera happened to catch them sitting in the stands, he'd always mention them by name. They knew him, they grew up here, they knew how famous he was. And when I talk with them about Harry, you can tell they feel like a big part of their childhood is gone.

I'll bet a lot of people feel that way.

We're in a position here, when you work with the Phillies, to be around a lot of famous people. But there's a lot of people here who don't get to know the players, don't get to know the coaches. But I'd bet just about everybody got to know Harry in some way—knew him, liked him, probably had a beer with him. He embraced everybody like they weren't any less important than the boss.

I was fortunate enough to go to Cooperstown when Harry got inducted. And he did such a great job. That year Ozzie Smith went in, too, and for me that was a big day. To see him there, that was one of our friends. That wasn't some guy up on a pedestal; that was someone we knew and loved. He was such a special person. We threw this big party, and we were afraid Harry wouldn't be able to make it—they keep the inductees pretty busy, there are a lot of parties, and Harry is rubbing elbows with all the Hall of Fame people—but at some point people started whispering that his son Todd had called and he was going to make sure Harry got to the party. We all thought that was great news. Everybody just waited for him to show up, and he did, and he sang "High Hopes" and it was just great. I just can't tell you how special that was.

Of all the things I've been lucky enough to do—and I've been very lucky in this life—to look up there that day and see all those giants of the game line up behind Harry . . . that was pretty good.

FROM THE FIELD OF SCREAMS AND THE LAND OF AHS

Larry Costigan

Larry Costigan realized a childhood dream by working with Harry Kalas. Costigan grew up in Haddonfield, New Jersey, listening to almost every Phillies game. After earning double degrees at Seton Hall, Costigan, 35, became a producer for Westwood One Communications.

I grew up in South Jersey, wanting to be Harry! There's never anything negative to say about Harry Kalas. I've been working with him for 10 years. You have difference of opinion with announcers and difference of philosophies, but with Harry, I couldn't tell you one bad thing about him. He was an absolute dream to work with. I started doing this when I was 25 years old. Because he was a childhood idol of mine I was extremely nervous, wondering what he was going to be like, very intimidated. With Harry, he made it seem like I had been his producer for 30 years. He just hit the ground running with me. He had absolute trust—that's the big thing with a producer and an announcer—you gotta have that mutual trust. With Harry, it was right there from the beginning.

I grew up five minutes from Philadelphia—Eagles, Phillies, Flyers, Sixers! Philadelphia is unlike any other city. The fans love their sports and identify with their announcer more than any other city I've seen. I travel all over the country doing what I do. With the Phillies, Mike Schmidt came and went . . . Pete Rose came and went . . . but there was always Harry Kalas.

Announcers used spotting boards and scorecards. I was at a 49er football game with Harry in San Francisco once. We were all the way at the top of the stadium. It was a very windy day at Candlestick Park. The game gets under way, and Harry has his spotting board right there in front of him on the counter. A big gust of wind comes into the booth, blows his spotting board out the window. For an announcer—that's his lifeline. It's where he had all the players, the depth charts and everything. But Harry Kalas was so well prepared, he knew every number and every name on the jersey, that he did the rest of the game without the spotting board and you couldn't even tell. He was so well prepared. A lot of guys we work with will have notes on the counter and little tidbits on the players so if it comes up in the broadcast, they can fill you in with details . . . but Harry knew it all. He just did his homework before he got to the stadium so all he needed was the spotting board, and he had a story or a note on every single player. He didn't have to look at his notes to have it. That's how well prepared he was. He was "old-school."

> . . . he had a story on every single player. He didn't have to look at his notes . . . He was "old school."

One of Harry's old partners was Jack Ham. Jack would walk into the booth with no notes, no press guides, no anything, no spotting board. But Jack was great. He was like, "I'm not going to tell you what's in the press notes. I'm going to watch the game and tell you what I'm seeing." That was Jack's style. That's why he and Harry were great. Harry had all the information and could paint the picture . . . Jack could tell you "this is why they did what they did, why they're running that defense." That was another good quality about Harry. He worked with different partners over the years, and he seemed to always bring out the best of the guys he worked with.

In radio, there are no pictures. Jack could explain things. He'd say there's a 4-3 defense. Well, people who are sports fans, they know what a 4-3 defense is. But Jack would explain, "This is why they're playing a 4-3 defense. This is why they're blitzing Tom Brady on every down here." He would explain it. Bob Trumpy was very similar when he did Sunday Night Football a long time ago. He was more of "I'm going to tell you." Their attitudes were that little tidbits and press notes are good, but I'm a former player and that's why you hired me to tell why teams run the plays they run and why they do the things they do. Jack was the same way. They'd go to practice on Friday. They'd talk to the coaches so they knew the game plan. There's instant credibility when an announcer can walk down to the field before the game and talk to the coaches. They'll give them information that they wouldn't give to me, as the producer. They don't know me at all . . . but they knew the announcers.

I've been doing this job for 10 years. The first couple of years, we did games in Veterans Stadium, which was a complete hole-in-the-wall, but it was neat.

My father passed away last year. One of the first games I did was with Harry Kalas. I got my dad a press pass and brought him to the game. Harry's announcing would annoy my dad because he thought Kalas would over-exaggerate things. I bring my dad to the game and introduce him to Harry. Harry was a big-time smoker, as was my dad. We get to a football game 3-4 hours ahead of time, so Harry and my dad are talking. By halftime, I said to my dad, "What do you think of Harry?" He said, "The greatest guy in the world." It turns out they were going out for smoke breaks and shooting the breeze. That's another example—you could meet Harry once and any perception you may have had beforehand would be out the window. For me to get to do an Eagle game with Harry Kalas in Veterans Stadium was wonderful.

There are only two people in all of the games I've done—the NCAA tournament for seven years, all the football games I've done—that I've ever been intimidated in working with: Harry Kalas and John Thompson. With those two guys I got a little intimidated, a little nervous, had to pinch myself and say, "I can't believe how great my job is."

It was always Philly for me because I grew up near Philadelphia. It was a neat, surreal feeling to be handing him cards, telling Harry Kalas when to go to a break, handing him a note about a player. It was neat. He's the reason I got into this business—I wanted to be him.

When I was in college, I was on the air, as an announcer, and I graduated and realized I probably didn't smoke enough cigarettes. I didn't have those pipes that Harry and a lot of those good announcers have. I ended up being a producer. There's no proof that smoking causes cancer. Well, there's no living proof.

On the radio, there are no directors. The producer does everything. On the television side, the director is the guy changing the camera shots—like in the truck telling them to go to different cameras. I like to think of the producer as more the guy who does the preparation before the broadcasts. He scripts out what they're going to do in every segment, what they're going to talk about, how long they have in every segment. The director is more the "live" guy. Once the broadcast starts, he's dealing with the camera and the production people, and the producer is dealing with the announcers. In radio, being that we don't have a director, you manage everything from coordinating interviews with the teams earlier in the week for your announcers to talking on the phone with the players from each team. Making sure everyone on your crew has their proper credential, parking pass. Coordinating with your announcers when they get into town.

All the old-time guys are humble. They started doing this when this business wasn't as big as it is now. They're like the old-school athletes. They didn't make as much money back then. They appreciate everything a lot more.

Harry was a great storyteller. You would be captivated when he would tell you a story. There was a place we'd go in San Francisco, Lefty O'Doul's. Harry would go in. They'd all know him. It was a piano bar. Harry would take over. He'd stand next to the piano. He'd call me over, and I'd stand there with him. He would get the microphone. The girl would be playing the piano, and Harry would sing, "God Bless America," "Edelweiss" from *Sound of Music*, and the whole bar would be singing along. He's such an outgoing guy. People would say, "Who is that guy?" Unless you were in Philly, you knew the voice, but you probably didn't know what he looked like. What an absolute joy it was to work with Harry Kalas.

THE BIG BOPPER

Bill Giles

Bill Giles is the chairman and part owner of the Phillies—and the man who brought Harry Kalas to Philadelphia. Giles, the son of former National League president Warren Giles, began his baseball career with the Reds and worked in Houston in a variety of roles—but always with an eye on generating publicity, often with wacky stunts. It might be said that Giles' greatest public relations coup for the Phillies was hiring Kalas to be the team's lead broadcaster in 1971.

I was the marketing director with the Houston Astros, and we had a radio/television division run by a gentleman named Dick Blue. We were in the market for a new announcer. Harry had sent his tape in from when he was working with the Hawaiian Islanders, and Dick Blue hired him to do the play-by-play in Houston, sharing it with Gene Elston. I had nothing to do with hiring him in Houston—but I got to know him quite well because I was the marketing guy and I was involved with the broadcasters. Harry and I became good personal friends, and he and his first wife Jasmine and my wife became friendly.

When I came to Philadelphia, we switched beer sponsors from Ballantine beer to Schmidt's. Schmidt's was paying us a million bucks a year as the main beer sponsor. They said they would not do it if Bill Campbell was one of the broadcasters. Bill Campbell had been doing a lot of Ballantine beer commercials, and Schmidt's didn't want Campbell around if they were going to pay us a million bucks. I decided to replace Bill Campbell—even though he was very popular at the time—because I knew that Harry would probably do a better job in the long term. I got to know him personally, and everybody liked Harry. He was very highly thought of as a broadcaster and as a human being.

He really knew his baseball. Just talking to him after the game all the time, he was very knowledgeable. When I fired Campbell, I had two guys on my list—Harry and Al Michaels, who was in Cincinnati. It's been said that Al Michaels might have been the first choice, but honestly I don't think I ever talked to Michaels.

I don't really remember how bad it was—but it was not a popular decision at the time. A lot of people liked Campbell. I don't remember it being too bad. I do recall that Campbell was very mad at me and never understood why I fired him. I did tell him, but I don't think he ever wanted to understand it.

> When I fired Campbell, I had two guys on my list—Harry and Al Michaels, who was in Cincinnati.

I always felt from the beginning that he was going to be accepted. It would just take a little time. Really, I never dwelled on it. When he went to work with Richie, that just made it so much better. I had no idea at the time that he and Richie were going to hit it off—both in the booth and out of the booth—as well as they did.

The most fun thing was, I played a lot of golf with the two of them. Harry gave me my nickname, the Bopper, which I still use. I used to hit the ball a lot farther than either Richie or Harry. We were playing one day and I hit a particularly long shot, and Harry says, "Bill, you're a real bopper with that driver." And that was it—that became my nickname.

Richie didn't like to look around for the sprinkler heads to tell him how far he was from the green on a particular shot. He'd always ask Harry, "How far am I, Harry? Dammit, how far am I?" and Harry would tell him. Richie would reach into his bag and say, "I have the perfect club for this shot." And consequently he'd hit a bad shot and he'd say, "Oh, Harry, you gave me the wrong club."

We had the two of them do a lot of silly things. We had them in a tricycle race one time—and Harry beat Richie. Then I asked them to do an Ostrich race. And that was the biggest blunder ever.

We put a sulky cart behind these two ostriches. This guy that had the ostriches convinced me that these ostriches would run peacefully around the warning track of the field, and we could have a nice little race. Harry and Richie were not excited about doing it. But I finally talked them into it. They started to get into these sulky carts—and the ostriches ran wild. They went wild. Both Harry and Richie ended up on the ground, and one of the ostriches ran up into the stands, and one of them ran loose around the field. Both guys were scared to death. They actually turned white. I said, "Whitey, I've never seen you so white."

It just happened with Harry and Richie. There was no design, no plan. The only thing I would tell them was: *Make it fun. Make it fun in the broadcast booth. Make sure you get a sense of humor in there once in a while.* Richie would say, "Don't worry about it, we'll take care of it." Richie told Harry, "Now, let me warn you— if there's nothing for me to say, I'm not going to say anything. You just keep talking. If something is worthwhile, I'm going to say my piece." Harry carried the ball without Richie sometimes because of the way Richie was. He didn't believe in talking just to be talking.

I remember the Ashburn church service, where Harry gave the eulogy. Harry really handled it well and kept his composure, for the most part. I lost it at the end and started crying. Harry was a pretty religious guy. His father was a preacher. Harry talked a lot about religion. He had some nice and very religious thoughts in his comments at the church.

He didn't have as much fun after Whitey passed. He loved his work, he loved doing it, but I don't believe—well, I know—that he didn't have as much fun in the booth as he did when Whitey was there.

My memories of Harry on a personal basis were really in spring training. His kids stayed in a condo right next door to where my family stayed. We had many fun times playing games, and Harry would always be the chairman of those games. We had a lot of fun with our boys in those days.

And of course, the dog track. Harry loved going to the dog track. One time we were coming home, and his wife Jasmine—she called him "Daddy"—said, "Daddy, it's embarrassing to see a grown man lose $300 at a dog track." Harry said, "Jasmine, I did not lose $300. I lost $600."

I'll never forget that. I laugh at that even now.

That's how we knew he wasn't feeling well this spring. He would always go to the track, but he didn't go much this year.

For years, network agreements prevented local announcers from calling the World Series. Only national crews could do it. In 1980 when we got to the World Series, Harry and the rest of our broadcasters couldn't do the games. I was very involved in changing that after 1980. We got so much heat—well, baseball did, not particularly the Phillies—from the local fans not being able to hear their broadcasters. I spent a lot of time talking to ABC and **NBC*** and major league baseball, and finally talked them into doing what they do now.

When I was in position to make trades, I'd ask him—because he would see more people in person than I would. I'd say, "When you interviewed this player, what kind of guy do you think he is? Do you think he's a straight-shooter? Do you think he has good character? Do you think he has bad character?" I would ask him quite a bit about the makeup of people he'd interviewed in those pre- or postgame shows, and I'd use him as somewhat of a scout, actually, on the player as a person. Harry always had a pretty good read on people.

***NBC** Sports president Dick Ebersol recently paid $50,000 at a charity auction to have Carly Simon tell him the name of the subject person in her song, "You're So Vain." Only Simon, Ebersol, and that person know the identity, rumored to be Warren Beatty, James Taylor, or Mick Jagger.

Fanecdotes

When I got the phone call and they told me Richie Ashburn had died, my first thought was, "Oh my God—Harry. What is he going to do?"

We had a public viewing on a Friday, and Vice President of Media Relations Larry Shenk told me to videotape it and to shoot the private funeral when Harry gave the eulogy. I went to tell him I'd be there; I didn't want him to look up and see the camera rolling if he didn't expect it.

I find him sitting by himself in the lunchroom—which was rare enough; Harry was never sitting by himself. I walked over and told him what I'd be doing, and it occurred to me as I was talking that he wasn't hearing a word I was saying. Finally he looked up at me and said, "I have to give my best friend's eulogy, and I can't do it. I've got 10 hours, and I can't do it. I gave my father's eulogy, and it wasn't as hard as this. I've written it three times, and each time I've thrown it away. I've got 10 hours, and I have to give the eulogy for my best friend. And I can't do it."

> Finally he looked up at me and said, "I have to give my best friend's eulogy, and I can't do it.

And he got up and walked away. I have never felt so bad for anyone. His heart was just broken, and I showed up the next day and the camera is rolling and I had no idea how he'd get through it.

That morning, he was so strong. He was incredible. He got everybody through it. He got us all through it. He was awesome. I was so moved; I wrote him a letter telling him how proud I was, and telling him what a great job he did. I couldn't even talk to him about it; I just wrote it down. I knew how hard that was for him. And he sent his friend off perfectly.

I asked Harry to introduce our wedding party, as a lot of people did, and he agreed—as he always did. So he's doing our intro, and he says:

"Before we begin the ceremony, let's all hold hands together and say a prayer for our troops in Operation Desert Shield. They're so far away from their loved ones . . ."

And on and on he goes. He had everyone holding hands and sending a prayer overseas to our fighting men and women. And because it was Harry, everybody thought it was great. Anything with soldiers, firemen, cops, Harry was always moved by those guys.

He was big on holding hands together and singing. At one Christmas party Harry gets up and says, "Let's all hold hands together and sing the greatest song ever written about Christmas." And he sings "Silent Night." And it's great. But no one knows the second verse to "Silent Night." Except Harry. He knew all the words to every song ever written. He starts singing the second verse, and we're all going, "Mmmmm . . . Mmmmm . . . Mmmmm . . ." humming along. Half of us were laughing, and half of us were shushing them, saying, "Harry will get mad if you laugh during 'Silent Night'—it's the greatest song ever written about Christmas."

Harry used to go to the senior citizens' place to sing Christmas carols every year. He'd always tell them the only song he wouldn't want to sing was "Jingle Bells." I don't know why; he didn't think it was Christmas-y enough. And every year one of the senior citizens would ask him to sing "Jingle Bells." And he'd just shrug, and he'd always do it. He never said no to anybody.

—**Dan Stephenson**, Phillies videographer

People would constantly show up and ask if they could just say hello to Harry. They didn't really need a conversation, they didn't want anything from him, they just wanted to say hello to him. They always felt like they knew Harry, people always felt like they were friends with him. And I'd always have to go ask him, and he'd always say: "Sure. Bring 'em in." I never saw him turn anyone down. I never saw him mad or in a bad mood. He was great to everybody, all the time. That's the way he was: "Sure. Bring 'em in."

—**Art Cassidy**, longtime Phillies pressbox attendant

I was an intern in the Phillies public relations department and I actually thought I would only last one year, so I wanted to get a photo with Harry before I left. The problem is, the camera was so old, that the picture came out terrible and I never had another picture taken. All I have is this horrible, grainy photo taken in 2000.

I remember the first time he walked into the PR department. I was awestruck because it's Harry Kalas. The one thing that stood out was I was an intern and how good he was to me. He treated me the same way he treated Larry Shenk who had been there for 40 years and I had been there three months.

The thing I've always said about Harry is, he's the last man on the planet to look for the bad in people. We are such a cynical society; that cynicism didn't live in Harry. He didn't judge anybody. He accepted everybody and liked everybody. He was the last person on earth to look for the bad in people.

One day we're in the PR department, it's a Saturday and we're on Fox. At the time, Mary Ann Gettis, now the coordinator of marketing initiative, was working for us and she handled all of Harry's mail. Harry was in there working in her little cubicle. Now, Karen Nocella is walking through the PR department and the elevators open up and Tim McCarver from Fox walks out. Now, understand that Tim knows Karen. He knows her name is Karen but for some reason he walks off the elevator and says "Rebecca!" And Harry, who is walking past them, with a cup of coffee in his hand staring straight ahead, never breaking stride, simply says in that voice, "Close enough," and just kept walking. He had such great timing and deadpan that it was hysterical. There's no doubt that every time Harry saw Tim he asked how Rebecca was.

Let me tell you something: Harry loved my last name. He loved long, ethnic names. Willie Montanez, Mickey Morandini, Ricky Bottallico. I'm a Casterioto. From the day I started until the day he passed away—he saw me that morning—he said "Greg Cas-teri-otto." In nine years, it never got old. Brought a smile to my face every time. He said it the same way, every time. I used to tell people that he wished I played. He loved the names he could punctuate.

We were in Miami, and Harry wanted the stats for the next team we were playing. He wanted them early because he wanted to prepare. So he calls my room, "Greg, HK here." I said, "Yeah, Harry, how can I help you?" And it's not like I couldn't recognize that voice, but that was Harry. So he asked me for some stats and I said, "I'll run them up to your room." He tells me not to worry, that he was heading to the pool and he'd stop by my room. So I hear the knock at the door and I know who it is and I open the door and here's Harry. It was the coolest thing I ever seen. It was like I went back to 1950 Hollywood. Here's this golden tanned man. He has his hair slicked back, a cigarette behind one ear, an aqua terry cloth waist jacket and matching pants with shower shoes. It was the coolest look I've ever seen. I love Sinatra and it was like I was looking at Sinatra. He oozed '50s cool. He did. It dripped off of him. I would tell Todd Kalas in spring training whenever I'd see him, "Do you know how cool your dad is?"

I miss Harry right now and my one regret is I didn't spend more time using those moments just to talk to him more. It's not often you can just sit and talk to someone like Harry, and I look back and wish I had more moments like that to relive. He was just a great, great person.

—**Greg Casterioto**, Phillies public relation staff

Well, for me personally Harry helped me to understand, even after I had been a coach and then up to the booth, that this is a new age. That this is a different era in baseball and to look at a bigger picture when analyzing this team or any team for that matter. He showed me that a Ryan Howard striking out was not that big of a deal. He taught me to look at the other part of it. Ryan's other numbers, when taken as a whole, far outweigh the strikeouts. Harry recognized that long ago. I had a tendency of being overcritical at times of guys striking out and not moving the ball. We couldn't have won this last year without Ryan Howard. Harry would point out that he's still young and learning how to hit. Don't be too critical and don't forget that it's a difficult thing to hit a baseball; he would remind me of that constantly.

Harry would tell it the way it was, like that ball should have been caught but he wouldn't dwell on it. He wouldn't go back to it late in the game.

Sure, he knew the game, but Harry had a different perspective than I have or for that matter, Wheels has. I can look out there and see a guy fouling off pitches and fouling off pitches and look to second and know the guy out there is tipping pitches. Or if a guy is getting lit up, I can tell if he's tipping his pitches. That's not what the play-by-play man is going to focus on or even worry about. It's a different job.

—**Gary "Sarge" Matthews**, Phillies player ('81–83) and broadcaster ('07–present)

When I first got to Philadelphia, Lenny Dykstra had broken his hand and I got to play the following day in centerfield. It's my Phillies debut, which was a dream come true for me, obviously. Well, I had two doubles and a home run in my first game with the Phillies. Harry came down after the game and said, "Congratulations on your first home run. Here's the call."

Then he handed me a tape—the tape of him calling my home run. I still have it, to this day. When I was struggling, I'd play it. It's a great pick-me-up tape. I'm just so, so grateful that he'd think of me like that. And it's the perfect call: "Swing a long drive to left field, that ball is outta here!" And then Harry says: "What a debut for Ruben Amaro!" I still get chills when I hear it.

Here's the strange thing: My nephew Robert is now a college baseball player. My mom used to babysit for him when he was little, and one day she played that tape. And she said Robert just shuddered when he heard Harry's voice saying my name. Everytime we were over, we'd play that tape—and Robert would get this big smile on his face and start bouncing up and down.

My nickname—the Total Package—was perpetuated by Mitch Williams. It was my nickname from '92. You know how Harry loved nicknames. I swear this is true—until the time of his passing, every time he greeted me, it was "Package . . . Total." Every single time. "Package . . . Total."

Even when I became the assistant GM, Harry would introduce me at whatever function we where at with "The Total Package, Ruben Amaro." The PR staff at some point had to say to him, look, this guy is an executive now, he's the assistant general manager of the club, maybe that's not quite the way we should introduce him. He stopped doing it; he would never embarrass anybody, he didn't mean any harm by it. But he never stopped greeting me with "Package . . . Total."

—**Ruben Amaro, Jr.**, Phillies outfield, 1992–93;
assistant general manager, 1996–2008

In the '80s we would go on a winter press tour to Lancaster, Wilkes-Barre and Reading, and do banquets. You're riding busses around from city to city, and someone would say, "The players are hungry; let's pull over and eat." So we'd pull into these fast-food places, and all of a sudden you'd hear Harry, "How 'bout a cheeseburger, large fries and a vanilla milkshake?" He even made ordering fast food sound magical. Just his voice would bring the place to a dead stop.

> He even made ordering fast food sound magical.

He treated everybody's name as something unique. It was interesting when I saw Todd Kalas (Harry's son), I guess it would have been four or five days after Harry died; he greeted me as Vinnie. Very few people call me Vinnie; I guess because I'm not Italian. Harry would always greet me as Vinnie Nauss. It was interesting to have your name called by Harry Kalas.

He's done answering-machine messages for a long time. The first time I can remember is back in the '80s. People who worked for the Phillies would say, "Can you leave a message on my answering machine?" And they would ask on behalf of others. So he'd say: "Joanne can't come to the phone right now, because she went out FOR A LONG DRIVE . . . ."

It's hard to say how often he did that. Back in the early to mid-'80s was the first time I ever became aware of it. Employees would come in and ask. I would say it was occasional. But then I just heard a number of people tell that story about being somewhere—at a function away from the park or at the ballpark—and seeing a fan say to Harry, "Hey, would you record this into my cell phone?" I'm not a techie, but I guess they could somehow put it on their answering machine. Going back 25 years or so, I guess it was one thing that he did it for coworkers. But then to hear how he used to do it for strangers, and to hear it from quite a number of different people, seemed like it was probably frequent, I would say.

—**Vince Nauss**, 50, was a Phillies publicist from 1983–89. He now serves as president of **BASEBALL CHAPEL***, which provides chaplains throughout major and minor league baseball.

It was in spring training, and I think it was Harry's first year here. I remember being out at the batting cage and Mike Schmidt and Greg Luzinski were just crushing balls and I kept saying, "That ball's outta here." I didn't say it like Harry, no one could, but I just said, "There's another one outta here." He just looked at me and he didn't say anything. A little while later, I was listening to some replays and I heard him saying, "Outta Here! Michael Jack Schmidt." I'm thinking, hey, that sounds pretty good, and I knew I could never do it that well. That's how it started.

***BASEBALL CHAPEL** was started in the 1960s by Detroit sportswriter Watson Spoelstra as thanksgiving for his daughter surviving a near-death situation. His grandson, Erik, is head coach of the Miami Heat.

No question, his positive nature stood out more because at times this city can be negative. But even at banquets, he'd be positive. In the early '70s, we'd go on those caravans and we were terrible, but Harry'd always say, "This is the year the Fighting' Phils are going to break out," and I'd look around and think, what's he talking about? We were still really young and had a ways to go, but not in Harry's mind, and he really believed it. Every year, he would do the same thing. In the mid-'70s when we got real good, he just took it to another level. But if you listened to him at banquets, no matter where we finished, fourth or sixth or whatever, he'd be positive. I did a lot of those banquets with him in the winter. He wouldn't care, I'd get frustrated, but I don't want to say it's a company line because then you can make a mistake. But it was his line and he meant it.

I remember when Steve Carlton won 27 games. Lefty always said, "Today's win day, boys," and we had 100 losses and we'd say, "Yeah, all right." Harry would come in and say the same thing, "Today is win day, boys, Lefty is going." It was always like that.

We'd bus it to New York and talk baseball. In a bar after a game, it was baseball. It was never the economy and in the '70s the economy wasn't too good. It was always baseball, and he'd always ask questions about different players. You know, "Can this guy play?" and I'd say, "No," and he'd come back, "Yes he can. He can pitch." But he'd go through the whole league and ask you about every guy. He never wavered on his opinion. Lot of times, with other announcers, they'll just agree with you or a player, but not Harry. If he thought a guy could play and you didn't, he'd stick to his guns. He always thought everyone on the Phillies could play, but you could debate other guys in the league. But if you were with the Phillies, no matter who you were, if you just got called up from Triple-A, you could play. He could be 0-for-18 and he'd say he had a nice swing and it was just going to take time. "He'll be all right."

—**Larry Bowa**, Phillies shortstop, 1970-81, and manager, 2001-04

Harry got a kick out of the Phanatic. He always saw the value of the Phanatic as a great ambassador for the team. He saw players come and go and he liked the fact that the Phanatic was the one guy who isn't going to be traded to the Mets. No question, Harry had a love for the Phanatic.

We used to do a lot of appearances together. Certainly in the off season, sometimes it's hard to get the players, and since Harry lived in the area, we did a lot of appearances together over the years. Every year, we would visit a nursing home at Christmas and he'd sing Christmas carols and the Phanatic world dress as Phanta Claus. Also, the Veterans Administration every February when they had an appreciation week. Harry was the straight man and he knew how to work the Phanatic. They were a great comedy team.

The broadcasters in general love "The Streak." When the Phanatic takes off his shirt and Dan Baker announces, "Anyone entering the field will be ejected and anyone foolish enough to streak will be prosecuted to the fullest extent of the law," and then there's the streak music and out comes the Phanatic, I knew Harry would always laugh.

I think he always assumed the Phanatic had a screw loose and that's the way he was going to be. Harry was a true pro; he would roll with the punches. He was a big fan of Smiley the Pig as well, so he put up with us every Hatfield Dollar Dog Night. We'd bring in those hot dogs, and he'd love it.

—**Tom Burgoyne**, spokesman for the Phillie Phanatic

As a kid, I loved Bill Campbell. He was my favorite announcer. He was a real homer, which you're not supposed to be. I loved his excitement. I could give you "for instances," play-by-plays—I just loved him.

When they announced the Phillies had fired Bill Campbell, I was very upset. After Bill Campbell went to Pittsburgh and Harry came in, it took a long time for me to like him. I kept trying to get the Pittsburgh signal from KDKA so I could continue to listen to Campbell. I was hoping for Harry Kalas to fail. But, like everybody else, I fell in love with Harry Kalas.

There was a groundskeepers' party every year, on the last Sunday of the regular season. It was held at the nurses' station on the second level. The nurses would hire a band, The Bowery Boys, or the Quaker City String Band, an award-winning band. They would have an area set aside for them to do a jam session. There would be food and drink. The climax was when Harry Kalas and the Quaker City String Band would march through the stands, go out onto the field, and do the Mummers' strut all around Veterans Stadium, on the Astroturf, and up at home plate. We'd still be out on the field, changing the field for football for the last time. Then Harry Kalas would sing, "High Hopes" at home plate. The fans would all have left and the groundskeepers and the people from the party would be the only ones left there. Harry also loved to sing "On the Way to Cape May" and "My Way."

At most of the Phillies' home games, we groundskeepers had the best seats in the house, right behind the tunnel. A lot of times, I would go in the video room, which was near our area, and keep Dan Stephenson, the video guru, company.

One time when I was in there watching the game, a couple of players were in there. One was Chris Brock. Harry was on the air talking about the game and referred to something about what's going on in the back of the plane. Harry said, "In the back of the plane, we had fun. Remember this, Larry." And, they were telling funny stories about what happened at the back of the plane. Chris Brock jumped up out of his chair and said, "What the heck's he talking about the back of the plane for? He shouldn't even be in the back of the plane. It's a privilege for him to sit back there. He should be up front with all the other support staff." Then he goes to Ed Wade, the general manager, and demands that he doesn't want Harry Kalas to sit on the back of the plane. Wade went to Kalas and told him he couldn't sit in the back of the plane any more, and Harry Kalas almost quit on the spot. He broke down and cried. A couple of road trips later, he

IT WAS A BALL

was back in the back of the plane again, but that's the sad story. That's how spoiled and immature these ballplayers are. One time during batting practice, there was somebody standing around the batting cage where they have all the retired numbers. Richie Ashburn was still living and was announcing the games. Richie said, "Who's that #1 hanging up there?" The current player didn't even know that it was Richie's number.

My main man was #15, Richie Allen. As a kid, I idolized him. He took a liking to us. Right away, I heard he was a good guy. The first time I ever met him was my first year: August 1971. The grounds crew was having a late lunch out at one of the picnic tables. He [Allen] was with the Dodgers at the time. In walked this guy, in a cream-colored leisure suit. He had a big Panama hat on. He opened up the door and goes, "Where's Vic?" He was looking for one of the groundskeepers for Connie Mack Stadium. He comes and sits down directly across from me and starts drinking. About half an hour before the start of the game, here comes Tommy Lasorda, who was coaching the Dodgers at the time. Lasorda yelled at him to get out of there and get down there with the team. As Richie's leaving, I said to an old ground-skeeper, John Godfrey, "Wimpy, he ain't going to play, is he?" He said, "What do you mean, he ain't going to play? Sure he is. He'll probably hit a home run, too." Sure enough, I'm out there raking a base or something five minutes before the game, and here Allen comes out of the dugout. Later in the game, off pitcher Barry Lersh, he hit the ball off the Liberty Bell in center field.

MOISES ALOU* was the nicest visiting player who came in. One year, he was hurt. He didn't dress, but he traveled with the team. He sat in the tunnel with us during the game. After he started playing again, he always remembered that. When he came back to town, he remembered that my boss was big on cigars, and he made sure to have a big box of Cuban cigars for him. Every time. He never forgot.

---

*With the Expos in 1993, **MOISES ALOU** hit six consecutive home runs over a span of four games.

I have a book out, *Hardball and Hardship*. Hardball for two reasons: one for the obvious—working in baseball—and the other one is because I go hard on a couple of other topics, such as sports-talk radio, instant replay, sports announcers, and football officials in a funny way. There are a lot of behind-the-scenes stories on the Phillies. I also tell about the big Philadelphia tradition here, the Mummers. People can get this book now from my blog, *www.frogcarfagno.com*.

—**Mark "Froggy" Carfagno**, Phillies groundskeeper for 33 years

Back at Veterans Stadium, Harry would stop by my desk in the PR office every day to get the lineups and he always had a joke or a witty comment. He used to always say "Never change a winner" if our lineup was the same as the previous day. Those little exchanges were the highlight of my day. As sentimental as I was about leaving the Vet, I was also sad because I knew that the set-up of our offices in Citizens Bank Park would not give me that same interaction with Harry on a daily basis.

Harry loved to tease me and one of his favorite topics was my record on the road. I didn't travel with the team as part of my job, but I would usually take one road trip a year and unfortunately, the Phillies often didn't do too well with me along, something like that didn't go unnoticed by Harry. One year, as the Phils were about to finish an 0-7 trip, Harry spotted me in the stands from the booth, pointed at me and gave the thumbs down, letting me know in no uncertain terms that the lousy trip was all my fault. Of course, he did it with a smile on his face, as always, and nothing pleased me more than to be teased by Harry.

When I was putting together the tribute to him for *Phillies Magazine*, I spent many hours going through our photo archives. As I sifted through hundreds of prints and slides and CDs, all of a sudden I would find myself humming "High Hopes." It was like Harry was right there helping me. It's still hard to believe he's gone, but I will always cherish the memories I have.

—**Christine Negley**, Manager of Phillies Publications

He'd always been upbeat. Every single day I knew him, he was upbeat. Yeah, maybe he lost a little fire when Whitey passed away, but he was still upbeat. You just miss having him around. I can remember being at hotels and early in the morning, he'd be downstairs having his coffee and a cigarette. You come out of the hotel now and you can't help but look. I'm an early riser and I still look for him when I go downstairs. He may be gone, but he will always be with us.

Recently, I wore the white shoes as a tribute to him. They were fine, they're still in my locker and they will remain in my locker forever. He never changed his style, and that was a great thing about him. Harry wasn't going to wear something because it was a fad. He was going to wear it because he stuck with what worked for him.

> He's still with us, even if he doesn't come to the locker room anymore.

He's still with us, even if he doesn't come to the locker room anymore.

—**Milt Thompson**, Phillies player and coach

I will say this, there are a ton of stories with Harry in which he wasn't the leader, but he was certainly involved. One time in St. Louis, we were staying at the Hyatt. We were drinking and Scott Rolen got this look in his eye that Scott would get every so often. You knew he was up to no good and that trouble was coming. It was the normal group, Harry, Larry Andersen, me, and later Rolen joined us. They decided that since Chris Wheeler wasn't out and—even worse—hadn't asked for permission to stay in, he should be punished. Harry always had his "broadcaster's bed check time," so off we go. Commando Rolen decides we are going to destroy Wheels's room. We order a cot to be delivered. He calls room service to get the cot, so we get behind the cot and follow it down the hallway. Scott's creeping along the wall, which was funny enough because there were like five or six of us. We weren't quiet and Harry was right there in the middle of it. Phillies Enterprises' Vice President Richard Deats is with us, and we get to Wheels's room. He opens it up and curses, and we all follow the cot in. Harry is just laughing and he never did anything, but he was always encouraging. Someone says something about water. They're all over Wheels about how cheap he is, so Richard Deats opens the refrigerator and hold up three bottles of water—you know, they were like $7 each—and dumps them on the floor saying, "Hey, Wheels, seven bucks, seven bucks, fourteen bucks," and Wheels got all mad, like Wheels does, and nobody wanted to leave. They just wanted to stay and torture Wheels. It was just one of those weird, but classic nights. Like we were going to be quiet . . .

We're in Montreal. I always did my notes for the next day first, and then I'd go down to the bar. When I got there, Harry is sitting with a friend of his named Duke. He calls out "Leelee, c'mon over." I sit down and after a couple of minutes, Harry excuses himself to the bathroom. Not a big deal, but he doesn't come back. I look out in the lobby and he's at the elevator and just shrugs his shoulders. He wasn't setting me up; he was using me as a decoy because he couldn't say "no" to anyone.

After a while, John Kruk and Dave Hollins come into the bar and Hollins is still in "Mikey-mode," that alter ego of his. They call me over and I excuse myself, but Harry's friend follows me. This guy is asking me if I want to go speed boating with him or something like that. Kruk tells me to stay right there, and Mikey Hollins tells him, "She's not interested." This guy doesn't back away. Kruk has to separate them, and we call it a night. All I could think was Harry is going to get us in the newspaper because two Phillies went to jail because Mikey beat some guy up because of the PR girl, and it's all because Harry left me in the bar. The next day, they got all over him. "Harry, why did you leave Leelee all alone down there with that guy?" and all he did was shrug his shoulders. He just giggled and thought it was the funniest thing ever.

Harry Kalas was a wonderful human being.

—**Leigh Tobin**, Phillies Director of Public Relations, 1987-present

Chapter Four

THE WRITE STUFF

Ray Didinger
Kevin Roberts
Paul Hagen

The Fourth Estate Doesn't Take the Fifth

IF YOU'RE LUCKY ENOUGH TO WORK WITH HARRY KALAS, YOU'RE LUCKY ENOUGH

Ray Didinger

Ray Didinger, 62, is a columnist and commentator for Comcast Sportsnet in Philadelphia, after spending 27 years as a sportswriter and 12 years as a producer at NFL Films.

What a total professional I thought he was. I know when I worked at the newspaper, I made some road trips, and I would see him at the restaurant or the bar. When I worked at NFL Films, I had the opportunity to really work with him. He did a lot of voiceover work. If you wrote the script, you would sit in the booth with him. Every year, each producer had to do one or two highlight films. For nine years I did the Jets, and the Jets would always ask for Harry. Some teams would say it doesn't matter, but the Jets were very, very specific that they wanted Harry. He did it better than anybody.

Watching him do voiceover work was watching a total professional. You'd give him the script, then he'd read it one time and say, "OK, let's do it. Let's roll." He rarely missed a line. He rarely had a "pickup," where he had to do it over again. His narrations were as smooth as his broadcasts. Some narrators, you have to walk them through it . . . Some narrators you have to direct. With Harry there was none of that. He would read it one time and get it. He never missed. He was flawless. He could take very ordinary prose and make it sound wonderful. He would take mundane writing and make it sound like angels singing. When I did a piece on Comcast SportsNet after he died, I said he took your words, mounted them on velvet and bathed them in light. He elevated them. He took them someplace you never thought they could go.

It wasn't easy work. His narration all fit in little holes in the film. You're coming off an interview and going to a radio call or sideline sound. You've got to get a line in, in 6.5 seconds. It was that specific, and Harry got it right every time.

When I was writing lines, I could hear his voice. I knew the pace at which he read, to the point that I hit it right on the button. He was just so consistent. It never varied. If there was anything wrong, you made the mistake.

Wednesday was *Inside the NFL* day. The show would run from the first week of the regular season, right through the Super Bowl. You knew which highlight package you had to do, and Harry would come in and narrate it . . . Every Wednesday at 9 a.m., there was Harry with his cup of coffee, ready to go.

He was just a total perfectionist. He demanded a lot of himself. He was punctual and on top of his game and prepared, and he expected you to be the same. If you weren't, he would let you know it. The only time I messed up on the job, we were between two buildings—half in the old building and moving into the new building, three or four miles away. Harry was going to narrate the Jets highlight film on a Tuesday. At noon, Harry came in to narrate. I was going to fine-tune the script. All of a sudden the phone rang, and the audio engineer said, "Don't you see the time? Harry's here. He's ready to go." I was looking at the clock on my computer. Over the weekend it was the daylight savings time change. I was an hour off. I thought I had another hour, and I didn't.

Harry was right on time, and I wasn't there with the script. Harry was sitting there at the mike with his legs crossed. I came in, and he gave me a look. "Harry," I said, "I'm so sorry." I was explaining about the clock on my computer and he said, "Raymond, I expected more from you." His time was valuable. He was always on time and ready to go.

Some guys have to re-record their lines four or five times. Harry never did . . . Harry would go through 10 pages of script, and he might have to re-do one line. It was a joy, working with the guy.

No one knew who he was when he took over as Phillies broadcaster. The only one who did was Bill Giles. There was a lot of support for Bill Campbell. There was a lot of criticism and some resentment by people who had grown up with Bill. There was a feeling of, "Who's this guy they're bringing in from Houston?" A lot of people that first year or so didn't like Harry. It was more like, they weren't giving him a chance. Philadelphia's funny that way. If you're their guy, they will cling to you. They're very loyal.

> A lot of people that first year or so didn't like Harry.

The fact is, Harry was as good then as he ever was. But he wasn't Bill. It took a while for people to accept that, for them to give the guy a chance. Once people did, they realized what they had—a guy in the mold of the great broadcasters. Not that Bill Campbell wasn't. Bill Campbell was a great broadcaster. Once people settled down and got over their initial resentment, they ultimately fell in love with the guy. It's funny when I tell people who are not from around here that he wasn't embraced by the city. That first year there was a lot of criticism. People were saying, "Who's this guy? Get him out of here." It was very unfair. He was a great broadcaster.

The other thing was, he was a very versatile announcer. He was a real good football play-by-play guy. He did radio for Westwood One. I remember one game two years ago. The Eagles were at home, and I was driving home, and flipping through the channels to Westwood One. It was Dallas–New England; Harry was calling play-by-play, and he was terrific. He was really, really good. I was driving home and thinking, "This guy is really something." This was a big, big NFL game, and he set the right tone, the right level of excitement. He had the formation right, the players right. He was setting up the color man.

He was a great, great broadcaster—and a real gentleman. The thing I remember is after Game Five of the 1980 NLCS, the Phillies and Houston, which was one of the greatest postseason series ever. It was right down to the wire. It was five games of baseball that left you wrung dry. When it finally ended, Harry and I were getting back to the hotel at the same time—the Shamrock Hilton . . . Harry said, "Raymond, can you believe they pay us to do this?" I'll always remember that. That really captured how he felt about his life. I can still see the look on his face and hear his voice saying that as we came through the doors.

We would needle Harry, because we knew how much Harry loved Mike Schmidt. We would say things about Mike Schmidt and get Harry going. One night the Braves were in town. Bob Horner was playing third base. The Braves had taken a couple games from the Phillies, and Horner hit a couple home runs. So we'd say we think the best third baseman is Bob Horner, hands down. You'd see Harry, his face getting red. He'd say, "You guys don't know what you're talking about." After a half-hour, Harry slammed his hand down on the table and said, "Michael Jack Schmidt is the best player in the game today." I can still hear him saying that. We finally got the rise out of him we wanted. At that point, we all went home. If you made any crack about Schmidt, you could get Harry's goat. That was a game we played.

A writer named Mark Whicker, he was always sparring with Harry. Harry was talking about seeing Schmidt play in a Pro-Am: "I followed Schmitty, and he was hitting the ---- out of the ball." And Whicker says, "Remember, there are no men on base in golf." And Harry got so mad, because that was Schmidt's reputation: He didn't hit with men on base.

THESE 7 THINGS ARE THE 10 REASONS TO LOVE HARRY KALAS

Kevin Roberts

Kevin Roberts was the Phillies beat writer for the Courier-Post *of South Jersey from 1997–2003, when he became the newspaper's columnist. His newspaper career began in Michigan, then carried him to Arkansas, then to Pittsburgh, PA, and finally to Philadelphia. He does not regret that he will never again hear Harry's famous voice snap "Kev!" upon seeing him because he still hears it in his head all the time.*

When I found out that Harry was banned from the back of the plane, I wanted to write it at the time, but Harry wouldn't talk about it. The team was winning, and there was no way Harry was going to pick a fight, there was no way he was going to come off looking like a distraction to the team. It was never about him. So I held the story . . . until the following spring.

That winter Harry got the word he'd won the Ford Frick award, finally getting the call for the Hall of Fame, which he'd deserved for years. So in spring training, Harry finally agreed to talk about it with just two reporters—me and Paul Hagen, the great baseball writer for the *Philadelphia Daily News*. We were plainly trying to shame the Phillies into righting this wrong and inviting Harry back to his traditional seat. Which they did. That was when it all went crazy with Scott Rolen and Larry Bowa, so it wasn't the biggest story of the spring. But it was my favorite story. I felt like we'd restored a little order to the universe.

I tried to get Harry to say something edgy about it, something negative about the players, but there was no chance. I'll never forget the way he brushed it off. He said, "I found that the Coors Light went down just as smooth in the middle of the plane."

But don't kid yourself—Harry was crushed. Crushed. I remember thinking it was really going to be a test of how much he loved the players. Could he still root for the team? Could he feel the same way about the guys? Could he love those players again, the way he always did? And of course he could, and did. Harry forgave them in five minutes.

My first year on the Phillies beat was 1997, which was of course the year Richie Ashburn died. It was my first real exposure to Harry as a person, not just a broadcaster, and I was just blown away by how he handled Richie's demise. It broke him in half. He had to do every interview, tell every story, read the poem he wrote, give the eulogy, narrate the video, emcee the tribute, all of it. And it broke him in half every time. The way he mustered up and did it for his friend, honestly, it was heroic in its own way.

> He said, "I found that the Coors Light went down just as smooth in the middle of the plane."

Whitey died the night after a game in New York, and they had to come right back and play the next day. Harry did a bunch of interviews at the team hotel with the beat writers, then had to do a bunch more at the ballpark. They were taking him to do an interview down the third base line with yet another pack of media, and he walked past me. He saw me and just said, "Kev." And he put his hand on my right shoulder and almost sagged. I didn't know what to do; wasn't my job to do anything, and even if it was I hadn't been around long enough to say anything like, "Sorry, Harry's not doing any more interviews," but I was honestly concerned that he wasn't going to make it. But then he straightened up and walked over and did it again. And he was brilliant, as always.

That night at the hotel, I was walking past the bar and saw Harry sitting there. There were a handful of people around, but in a way Harry was sitting by himself. Usually with Harry, it's a big party, but people were sitting on the periphery, like they were afraid to intrude.

Harry got such a kick out of the moment of silence for Richie. Shea

Stadium was right near the airport, so occasionally a plane would go overhead during the games and split the air with this deafening roar. Well, at the exact moment the crowd fell silent, a plane went by: BOOM. It was chilling. Everybody got goosebumps. I made it the lead of my story that night; it really struck me. Harry wondered how they got the plane to fly over at that exact moment, like they'd orchestrated it. I said, "No, it was just coincidence." Harry thought for a moment and said, "Ha! That was his Whiteness!"

At the end of the night, it's last call, and we're all just sitting there. Harry reached into the pocket of his sport coat and pulled out a baseball—it was the game ball from that night. The Phillies won, 1-0—and 1 was Whitey's uniform number. The players had given the ball to Harry. He held it up toward the ceiling, toward Heaven, I guess, and said, "This one's for you, pal."

And, yeah, well . . . the hotel bar. It's impossible to talk about Harry and not involve the bar. Harry liked to have a drink, or seven. In those years when the Phillies were dismal and just getting clobbered, Harry would walk through the pressbox saying: "See-through! See-through!" That was his announcement that it was going to take hard liquor—the clear stuff you could see through—to endure watching this nonsense.

Harry's life was weirdly blessed when it came to baseball. When Joe DiMaggio died, I approached Harry out of the blue to see if he might have crossed paths with him somewhere and have a story. Harry said, "I was Joe D's driver." When he was serving in the army, he was stationed in Hawaii, and one day there was a dignitary coming in and it fell to Harry to chauffeur him. And it was Joe DiMaggio. Stuff like that happened to Harry all the time.

Harry once told this story: When he was serving out his army hitch in Hawaii, he was in a bar one night talking with someone about what he wanted to do when he got out of the military, and Harry was saying he wanted to be a baseball play-by-play announcer. And around midnight, in walked Buddy Blattner, who was a broadcaster for the Giants, and Lefty O'Doul, a great major league player who was then managing in the minors. They were on their way to

Japan for a baseball tour, or coming from Japan, I can't remember, and they had a stopover in Hawaii. But Harry happened to be there and talked with Buddy Blattner and got a handle on how to go about being a broadcaster. Stuff like that. Blessed.

His first job was as a play-by-play announcer for the Hawaii Islanders, where he had to re-create the road games in a studio. Someone would call in the result—grounder to second—and Harry would just invent the scene. He used to say if the game got lopsided and the crew wanted to get across the street to the bar, he could move the game along faster. "We had a lot of first-pitch swinging some days," Harry said.

But those were all small moments. The big moment, that's where Harry was always great. After the 9/11 attacks, Harry—like every other broadcaster in every other city—had to begin the telecast by talking about it, by welcoming the fans back to baseball. He of course struck just the right tone, and he was fantastic. But I always thought his best work was done after the games in that first series against Atlanta when baseball resumed play.

At the Vet in those days, everybody would sit in the press dining room after the games, drinking beer, talking baseball, hanging out. And Sept. 17–19, the Phillies returned to the field by beating the Braves three straight. After every game, Harry led the room in singing, "God Bless America." Everybody stood. People wept. It was a heck of a thing. Of course, because it was Harry, and because the Phillies were fighting it out with Atlanta for the division title, he prefaced "God Bless America" by saying, "Screw the Braves." . . .

A writer at another paper once said to me, "I think it's time. I'm going to write that the Phillies should get rid of Harry." I said, "Go for it. I totally encourage you, I'm behind you 100 percent. And I wish you luck in your future endeavors, and I'll be there to hold your coat while the fans run you out of town." For me, that stuff was dumb.

You won't ever see another like him—in the booth, or out. I'm lucky to have known him.

WHY CAN'T SUGAR BE AS SWEET AS HARRY KALAS?

Paul Hagen

Paul Hagen, one of the most respected baseball writers in the country, is a former president of the Baseball Writers Associa- tion of America and has covered baseball since 1974 in California, Texas and Phila- delphia. He was the Phillies' beat writer for the Philadelphia Daily News *from 1987 until 2002, when he became the newspaper's national base- ball writer. He has been known on occasion to do a pretty fair Harry Kalas impression, usually over a beer or two.*

For our 10th anniversary, in 1991, my wife Karen and I decided to visit Sydney, Australia. We flew from Philadel- phia to Dallas, Dallas to Honolulu, and then Honolulu to Sydney. It took something like 22 hours.

Anyway, we were already pretty jet-lagged by the time we started the third leg of the trip. We were dozing off somewhere over the middle of the Pacific when I heard the voice. It was Harry's voice. I thought I must be dreaming. No, it was really Harry's voice. Then I figured it out. The in-flight entertainment was featuring a seg- ment from NFL Films and Harry Kalas was narrating it. We were literally halfway around the world and there he was. It was then I fully realized for the first time that he really was a big deal, more than just the Phillies' broadcaster that I saw almost every day from the beginning of spring training to the end of the season.

And the reason I'd never thought about it before that was because he was so humble, so down-to-earth, that it was easy to get lulled into thinking that he was no big deal.

Harry quit drinking four or five years before he passed away.

The fact that he used to enjoy a cocktail before that was hardly a secret.

In fact, one night a couple years after I first came to Philadelphia I was writing a story late in the year about how the Phillies, despite another losing season, thought they had a chance to be better next year. The lead to the story was something along the lines of: *Sometimes The Voice of the Phillies, when the spirits moved him, liked to sing "High Hopes."* And it went on to say that this was an appropriate sentiment for the organization going into the following season.

> ...somewhere over the middle of the Pacific when I heard the voice. It was Harry's voice.

I had just begun to worry that this might be a little too personal when I looked up in the back of the Veterans Stadium pressbox and noticed Harry walking by. I asked him to come down and look at what I'd written and if he had any problem with it. He just laughed. "No, I think everybody knows that," he said.

Anyway, one day the Phillies played an afternoon game in San Francisco, at Candlestick Park. At the end of the evening, a pretty decent crew was in the hotel bar when Harry walked in. Somebody asked him where he'd been since the end of the game.

He started rattling off a few places. A piano bar. The bar in another hotel. A couple more bars.

"But where did you have dinner?" he was asked.

Harry thought a moment. A look of genuine puzzlement crossed his face. Finally he shrugged. "I seem to have whiffed on dinner," he said.

I went to the broadcast booth to ask Harry a question before a game once. We were sitting there talking and somebody came in to remind him that he was supposed to do a voice-over of some sort.

He took the sheet of paper, glanced at it, and nodded. He turned to the microphone and knocked it out perfectly in one take, then turned back to me and picked up the conversation without missing a beat. It was one of the most impressive things I've ever seen.

He just always wanted to believe that, in baseball at least, everybody was wonderful.

Harry loved players. Absolutely loved the players.

A few of us were sitting around one night late in spring training—Harry, Larry Andersen, then still a player, and a couple of beat writers.

"Who do you think will win the fifth starter's spot?" Harry asked.

"I don't care as long as it's not a certain righthander," I replied. "I don't like him at all."

Harry seemed honestly stunned by this. "Really?" he said, almost beseechingly. "I always thought he was a nice young man."

"It's not just the media that doesn't like him," I said. "Even his teammates think he's a jerk."

This really threw Harry. He just did not want to believe it. It was just another example of Harry always wanting to see the best in everybody. Finally, he turned to Andersen. "L. A.! Can this possibly be true?" he asked.

Andersen never hesitated. "Yup," he said, taking a swig of his beer. The rest of us cracked up. But it really bothered Harry. He just always wanted to believe that, in baseball at least, everybody was wonderful.

You can't really talk about Harry without talking about Rich Ashburn. What I remember most about the day Whitey died while the Phillies were in New York playing the Mets was how devastated Harry was and how gracious he was to everybody who needed to talk to him.

The beat writers went to his room at the Grand Hyatt. Then, at **SHEA STADIUM***, he did another round of interviews for the television cameras. He called the game that night.

Afterward, an impromptu wake broke out at the hotel bar back at the Hyatt. Harry had a baseball in his hands, and he was gripping it and rubbing it as if it were some kind of good luck charm. He said it was the game ball and that the players had given it to him. You could just tell how much it meant to him.

This isn't an original thought, but it's true: As good as Harry was for the rest of his career, he was never quite the same after Whitey died. It was like a little piece of Harry had died, too.

Here's one of Harry's favorite Whitey stories:

"One of Whitey's responsibilities when he was broadcasting for the Phillies was doing the pregame show, taping an interview with an opposing manager or player or coach. He'd take his tape recorder down to the clubhouse and get an interview, and he'd come back up. He'd say, 'Boys, that might be the best interview I ever had.' He'd hand the tape machine to the technician and the tech would say, 'Whitey, there's nothing on here.' I mean, if this happened once it happened 50 times.

"And Richie would then have to scramble out of the booth, go find the first warm body and try to do an interview for the pregame show.

"So one night we're sitting in a hotel bar in New York and a blonde hooker came walking up to us. She said, 'Boys, I'll do anything you want for a hundred dollars.' Whitey thought for a while and said, 'How about the pregame show?'"

---

*During a 1979 game against the New York Jets at **SHEA STADIUM**, a remote control model airplane crashed into the stands at half-time, hit a Patriots fan and killed him.

Short Stories from Long Memories

I was in line at Wawa (a convenience store in suburban Philadelphia) one morning with my coffee, on the way to the airport for an Eagles road game, and Harry was about three back in line. I hadn't seen him. It was a typical sleepy morning for everyone there, and suddenly that voice boomed out: "Shouldn't you be in In-DEE-ah-NAP-olis by now?" And everyone jumped and looked at the ceiling and looked around, and there was Harry in his baby blue sport coat, holding his own coffee and snickering like he did: "Hneh, hneh, hneh." And what was great was that people didn't swarm him or make a big deal out of it. They all just laughed and said, "Hey, Harry." Just a regular guy from the neighborhood who happened to be a nationally known star.

—**Bob Ford**, *Philadelphia Inquirer* columnist

Joining a baseball beat is not unlike being sent to a small, private boys' school. This is true especially in the Northeast, and especially in Philadelphia.

Baseball writers comprise a closed society, one that requires years of loyalty and correct behavior before assimilation is complete. Even then, acceptance might never come.

Spring training was a lesson in social dynamics; learning how to dress, who to speak with, which writers led the packs, and, mainly, learning that you made your bones over time, period.

So on that first road trip, the klieg lights were on. It was every man for himself, as is the nature of the beat. The Phillies beat was one of the larger traveling beats; between six and 10 writers or columnists made virtually every trip.

. . . Which left about a 20-minute window, sometime between 6 p.m. and 7 p.m., in which the writers, broadcasters and Turner Field workers would eat in the press dining room. Like any cafeteria, this dining room was zoned: This group ate in this corner, that group in the big middle table, these two guys over there, etc.

I was the et cetera.

After paying, I sat in a side table with a window overlooking the concourse. It was a table for two, but I planned ahead and brought game notes and media guides. This way, instead of being alone, I would be busy. Working. Occupied, head down, preparing.

My plan collapsed when I saw a pair of white shoes glide into my downcast sightline and heard a soft baritone asked, "Mind if I join you?"

I did not. I had met Harry years before, and I had chatted with him during spring training, and while over the next seven years we would often break bread we had never been at the same table, much less shared a meal.

Eagerly, I stacked my papers and moved my drink. I spent the next half-hour listening to Harry the K talk about the flight down, Scott Rolen and Larry Bowa, the rainy spring training, how good the Braves had been for so long, John Smoltz as a closer . . .

Before I knew it, a producer was tapping Harry on the shoulder. It was showtime.

Harry apologized to the producer for being late, apologized to me for having to leave so suddenly, rose, and thanked me— thanked me—for having dinner with him.

—**Marcus Hayes**, 40, *Philadelphia Daily News*

Now, I've asked for one autograph in my life for myself. I've never truly appreciated the concept of autographs, but that's me and not a derisive shot at those who enjoy getting someone's signature. That said, Harry Kalas was my exception to the rule.

Growing up, I was also a fan of Notre Dame. I watched every game I could both in basketball and football and often heard the voice of the Phillies doing those games as well. In 1986, I was a freshman at the University of Dayton and the Irish came to town. At Dayton, we lived to beat Notre Dame. The Holy Alliance as it was called at the time included DePaul,

Marquette, Notre Dame and Dayton, and featured six games in total, and all the games were big. That said, when the Irish came to town, for us—if not **NOTRE DAME*** and its fan base—was the highlight of our year.

With that in mind, you can understand that the University of Dayton Arena went nuts when the Flyers beat Digger Phelps' Irish squad. Long before it became a fad and redundant, storming the court had to mean something and for us, this meant something. It meant something to me as well, and grasping my game program featuring Dayton power forward Ed Young, I charged the court as well. As I stood at center court, with a crowd of excited college students, I looked over at the scorer's table and saw Harry totaling up his scorebook. I walked over and called to get his attention. A security guard started to push me away, but Harry asked the guard to wait a second to find out what I wanted.

"I'm from Philly and would love to have your autograph," I yelled from the court.

"No problem, toss that program over here, young fella," Harry said in the voice from God.

Harry wrote on the cover, "To Mike, Great win for the Flyers. Harry Kalas.

—**Mike Radano**, former Phillies beat writer for the *Courier-Post*

With Game 6 of the '93 NLCS about to start, Harry and I just so happened to walk from the club's offices to the press box at the same time. But before one got to the owner's boxes and the broadcast booths, he had to walk through a little hallway that hovered over the main concourse. And when the masses below saw Harry walk by, they went nuts.

*Former **NOTRE DAME** quarterback Tony Rice has been on more covers of *Sports Illustrated* than Henry Aaron . . . when Aaron headed the Atlanta Braves minor league operations, he cut off the pockets on the players' pants so they couldn't carry tobacco products.

Rather than give a little wave like a guy walking the red carpet or some other type of celebrity, Harry pumped his fist, shouted to the crowd, and then launched into an impromptu call of the ninth inning that the fans all hoped was coming.

"Two outs, bottom of the ninth, two strikes on the batter . . . here comes the pitch . . . strike three, Mitchie-Poo struck 'em outta there! The Phillies are going to the World Series!"

The throng of people on the concourse below went crazy.

As it unfolded, Harry's little prognostication proved to be 100 percent accurate. . . .

It was a dreary December day, and my wife and I were driving home from Cooperstown, N.Y. (We're big "off-season" travelers—smaller crowds). After an hour or so of driving through upstate New York and Pennsylvania with little or no radio reception, we finally got a clear signal from a radio station carrying the Westwood One broadcast of a Pittsburgh Steelers game.

That meant Harry was doing the play-by-play.

Now, I really don't care much about the Steelers, and I wasn't particularly interested in the game, but since Harry was on the mike, it was a no-brainer.

Harry was driving us home.

The best part was, the Steelers had a running back named Chris Fuamatu-Ma'afala. It's not exactly a name that falls from the tongue, especially since the Steelers were giving the ball to Fuamatu-Ma'afala a lot that day.

But there was Harry, saying it over and over again with panache and that trademarked exaggerated pronunciation of his that made it sound like poetry.

"Chris Fu-AHma-tu MA-AH-faLAH!"

Over and over again.

Months later, when I saw Harry again at the Vet, I brought up the game and how we sat there in the car, just cheering for the Steelers to signal a play in for Fuamatu-Ma'afala to get the ball. Harry just smiled and pointed out how as an up-and-coming broadcaster in Hawaii, he delighted in saying Polynesian names and probably enjoyed calling that game as much as we enjoyed listening to it.

But when I tried and failed to say, "Chris Fuamatu-Ma'afala" just like Harry would, he stepped in and saved the name from my butchering.

"You mean that Chris Fu-AHma-tu MA-AH-faLAH," Harry said, doing his best Harry voice.

Loved it. Simply the best ever.

—**John Finger**, CSNPhilly.com Phillies beat writer

I invited Harry to my wedding in December 1997 and didn't get the RSVP, which was no big deal because I know he's a busy man and he travels during the NFL season for West-wood One radio network. A few days before the wedding, my phone rings and it's Harry.

"Brookie, it's Harry," he said—as if I wouldn't have known if he didn't tell me. "Can I still come to your wedding?"

Now, I'm laughing. Of course, I tell him he can still come. He was genuinely excited because he had learned that he was calling a game at Giants Stadium that Sunday, so he could come to my reception in Cherry Hill, stay in a nearby hotel and drive to the Meadowlands in the morning.

My wife and I weren't the headliners at our own wedding anymore, but that was OK. Harry was great, signing autographs and posing for photographs. He even sang "Thank Heaven for Little Girls" to my two-year-old niece. The highlight for my wife and me was when he introduced Mr. and Mrs. Brookover to the invited guests with that unmistakable call: "Brookie, your bach-elorhood is outta here!!!". . .

We were at Shea Stadium for a Saturday afternoon game and when it ended, Harry asked George King from the *Trenton Times* if he could give him a ride back to the hotel in Manhattan. King says he can, but tells Harry he has to write first. So while we're writing, Harry is drinking in the media lounge. Three hours later, we're done writing and Harry is feeling good.

On the way back to the city, we hit gridlock. Since we're well behind Harry drinking-wise, we decide to stop at a liquor store in a seedy part of Queens, which is probably redundant. While we're stopped, Harry notices two pit bulls barking behind a fence.

"I'll take care of these pit bulls," he says, before getting out of the car and barking at them. He was in no danger because the fence was about 20 feet high, but even his barks had a special tone to them.

And he says with a perfectly straight face: "In the middle of my best rendition ever of 'High Hopes,' this guy comes in and slits his wrists. In the middle of my best rendition ever."

—**Bob Brookover**, *Philadelphia Inquirer*

Harry did the forewords for two of my books. It was just for me a very enjoyable experience. He not only readily agreed to do it, but immediately agreed. He did it, and it was very nicely done. I was very appreciative of his willingness to do it.

One of my best memories is away from the field: My wife and I were going into the mall; Harry and I live fairly close. I saw him going into the mall, and I introduced him to my wife Lois. He was just so pleasant, like he knew Lois a long time.

Then we went in the mall, and I saw him after that. People kept coming up to him and wanting to talk. It wasn't just a couple people; it was a lot of people. He was just so nice to them. He talked, shook hands and signed a couple autographs. I couldn't help but think that 98 percent of the people on his level would have ignored them or brushed them off. But he didn't. He wasn't above any of them. They were all strangers, and he acted like they were long-lost buddies. People kept coming up to him. To me, it was real amazing. That was Harry. He was a nice, nice man.

Several things led Harry to win over the Philadelphia fans. Harry was a very down-to-earth guy. He didn't come into the booth like God . . . He just came in, and from a professional standpoint had a great voice, knowledge of the game and the ability to make good, accurate, interesting calls. That all brought people's attention. That's how he quickly caught hold.

Bill Campbell was an icon. Still is. There were so many great things he had done in his career. It was a shock to Bill when Kalas was given his job. But both of them handled it so professionally.

They've always been friends. There's never been any animosity. That speaks well of both of them.

My memories of Harry are just as strong from a personal standpoint. Like everybody else, I can't find anything really bad to say about Harry. They don't make people very often like him.

—**Rich Westcott**, has authored *The Phillies Encyclopedia* and 18 other books

My first year in town was 1994, working for a suburban newspaper, and we had our first child, a daughter, Mary; he announced it on the radio. It was such an honor to have Harry do that. Then one year we were talking in the Vet dining room, and it came up that we were going to have another baby due in October. And I said to Harry, "You won't be able to announce this one on the air, Harry. This one's coming in October." And he said, "Don't worry about that. We'll catch up with that kid in the World Series." I started laughing because the team was terrible; they weren't going to the World Series. But that was really typical Harry—even when the Phillies were on their way to the worst record in baseball, Harry was talking about the World Series. He just loved the Phillies, even in the tough times.

The Phillies used to have those really bad teams. I can remember during a stretch when they just could not close out a game. They had a kid named Kyle Kawabata who was saving a bunch of games in Clearwater. Harry would walk through the pressbox whenever the Phillies would blow a save and announce: "Just another save for that Kay-yuhl Kah-wah-bah-ta!" And really enunciate that great Hawaiian name; he loved names like that. And then he'd punctuate it by saying: "Bring him up!" He'd make you laugh with that, even when the team was so bad.

One of my greatest memories of Harry, sadly, will be that memorial service at the stadium. That was just unbelievable, the amount of people and the emotion. We'd had this horrible spring where it rained every day—but all of a sudden it decided it was going to be beautiful, blue skies and 80 degrees that one day. I looked out at that 2008 championship flag, and there was this light wind blowing out toward right—a home run wind, which seemed appropriate—and it kept that 2008 flag nicely spread out at attention that whole service. I know how much he loved calling that last out, and what a highlight that was in his career. And it struck me that the flag was at attention throughout the whole ceremony, and it served as a neat backdrop to certainly the most amazing memorial I've ever seen and one of the most amazing days I've ever seen.

—**Jim Salisbury**, *Philadelphia Inquirer*

Maybe 25 years ago, when my mother-in-law was in her 70s, I introduced her to Harry down in Clearwater; she had a winter home down there. It was the thrill of a lifetime for her. Then, when she went into a retirement home, she started a Harry Kalas Fan Club. He got her address and sent her a Christmas card and a birthday card every year until she passed away in her 90s. He'd call her Marge—his friend Marge. That's Harry.

We used to eat dinner in the press dining room a lot. If we ate dinner 500 times, we talked baseball 500 times. It was just automatic when we started talking that we would talk about baseball. We wouldn't talk about the weather or celebrities. It would always be baseball, all the time.

> If we ate dinner 500 times, we talked baseball 500 times.

My family gave me a surprise 75th birthday party two years ago, at the Palestra, which was a terrific experience for me. A lot of people came. Phillies executive Dave Montgomery came, people like that—Big Five coaches and so forth. And the Phillies were in Cincinnati . . . Harry was invited, but of course he was away. Harry being Harry, he took the time out, even though he was in Cincinnati, to send a message, congratulating me on my birthday—he always called me "Jackson"—and said some really nice words that Dan Baker read at this party. It was Harry again, thinking of somebody he really didn't have to think about. There he was, doing something nice again.

—**Jack Scheuer**, writer for 38 years, Associated Press

Back in the day, he was giving me errors in the press box for all those dropped foul balls . . . That all started in '84, believe or not. He made a celebrity out of me for all that. That all started on a Sunday afternoon, when a foul ball landed on the façade in front of the press box at the Vet. He was making a gesture at me, like, why didn't I catch that foul ball? Then the next pitch, son of a gun, that same batter hit a ball that went over my head. And then it just took off. I wasn't going to stick my hands out and try to catch a hard foul ball. It's amazing—you're a fan, sitting in the stands, you couldn't wait to get a foul ball. In the press box it was like, "no, thank you." It was the complete opposite.

I had one night where I went down to the manager's office—I think John Felske was managing the club then. I got a baseball and I had it sitting on a chair next to me. Harry walked into the manager's office, and I tried to cover it up. I thought this was going to backfire. Sure enough, the game starts, and after the first foul ball, he gives me the error sign. I took the baseball and started waving it up and down, like, "Here's the ball; I caught it." Harry said on the air, "Who's he kidding? He got that ball from the manager's office." I thought I could deceive him; it didn't work.

—**Skip "Memory Lane" Clayton**,
once associate publisher of *Phillies Report*

. . . My thoughts immediately went to when I finally got to meet Harry in person. After 21 years, it was almost as if I had known him forever. There were so many nights when it felt as though he was sitting on the couch next to me as he delivered his famous, trademark lines— "struck him out" and, better still, "Watch this baby . . . outta here." It was during the NL Championship Series last year when he introduced himself. I was talking to Fox baseball analyst Tim McCarver in the pressbox hallway when Harry came over and said hello in his singular voice—the one that made him sound cooler than Frank Sinatra on the chairman of the board's best day. Before long, a mischievous, little-boy smile spread across Harry's face.

"Did he tell you about Pat the Bait?" Harry asked as he nodded at McCarver.

That's how I learned that Pat Burrell—otherwise known as Pat the Bat—was called Pat the Bait during his first few years with the club. Kalas said that before Burrell was married, the older players used to drag him out to the bars—OK, so may be they didn't drag him, but you get the idea—so they could dangle him as bait to attract women.

"Can you imagine how many hearts Burrell has broken?" Kalas said. And we all had a good laugh.

It's impossible to explain how much that meant to me—standing there with Harry while he took the time to tell a story. It was like getting a gift that I never expected and wasn't worthy to receive.

The last time I talked to him was after the Phils beat the Rays and won the World Series. He and thousands of merry, tone-deaf backup singers had just finished singing "High Hopes" at Citizens Bank Park.

Harry was standing on the field with the players and front-office personnel and press. It was such a special night, and I just wanted to share it with him for a quick second. I went over and repeated the same thing I'd said to about 50 other people that evening: I waited my whole life to see a championship in the city, and I couldn't believe—after 25 long years—that it actually happened.

Harry nodded. His eyes looked a little red.

"It's a great feeling," he said. "You'll never forget this." We'll never forget you either, Harry. You were wonderful and you were ours and you will be deeply missed.

—**John Gonzalez**, *Philadelphia Inquirer* columnist

I don't remember the first time I met Harry but I remember the most fun I had with Harry. The most fun I had was when I was doing Angelo Cataldi's show on Comcast at Chickie & Pete's. We're hanging in the back room just hanging and talking. And Harry said, "Do you want to play some baseball trivia?" Sure, to play baseball trivia with Harry Kalas was an honor. It was like having a pitch-and-catch with Steve Carlton. So, he threw me a question; it was a great question. I think it was the last Phillies pitcher, developed by the farm system to pitch in the All-Star Game. I didn't know the answer and he laughed "No, Chris Short. Chalk one up for my side." I soon realized that he's getting a bit competitive. Not in a nasty way, but he's really enjoying himself. I threw him a question and I didn't want to start with a real tough one because, to be honest with you, I didn't want to embarrass Harry Kalas. I ask him and he hits it out of the park. I spent 15 minutes playing baseball trivia with Harry Kalas and had my butt absolutely handed to me but had a great time doing it. I saw not just his baseball knowledge, which nobody was going to question, but a playfulness and a competitiveness that I had no sense of. He loved it. When I'd asked him a question he'd say, "Oh now Glenbo, let me ponder that one for a moment and roll it around my head." I enjoyed those 15 minutes more than you could imagine.

I was there when Bo Schembechler became the Tigers president and tried to push out Ernie Harwell. "We have to go young, we have to go hip." It was such a miscalculation and the fans went absolutely nuts. It would have been the equivalent of that happening to Harry. Here there once were some rumors that came out like that. Our lines were filled with "are you kidding? Harry is an institution. He has the job as long as he wants."

I'm sure that Harry saw that he wasn't going to be doing this forever and the 2008 World Series was the opportunity to call something that hasn't happened since 1980. He savored every moment of it. I just saw him a little bit before games and you could see a little snap in his step and he was loving every moment of it. You could also tell that at this point, he was the face of the franchise and a national treasure.

—**Glen Macnow**, 610 WIP Midday show,
author of three books on Philly sports

Spring training 2005: I got an idea to do a column about Harry, about the beginning of his 35th season as the play-by-play guy. We talked for a while, and I asked him if he ever thought about retirement.

"I played with the idea," he said. "Then I thought, 'I still really enjoy doing the games.' When I'm not calling the games the way they should be called, the time will come to step away. But I don't think that time has arrived."

Toward the end of the interview, I asked him, "How are you able to retain the pitch and tone of your voice? I've read about singers using lemon juice and honey to try to maintain their voices. How do you do it?"

He didn't say anything. He reached into the lapel of the white collared shirt he was wearing, took out a pack of Parliament cigarettes and jiggled them.

—**Mike Sielski**, sports columnist for Calkins Newspapers

Just from being someone who listened to Harry long before I met him, I always knew how powerful his presence was on the franchise. But I'll never forget the moment that really drove the power of that presence home.

It was the day in 1987 that Mike Schmidt hit his 500th home run. I was covering that game, so I didn't hear that call live, of course. But as Schmitty rounded the bases, I remembered thinking (as I so often did), I wonder how Harry called THAT one. For those of us who spent years listening to Harry before we covered the Phillies, that thought was always in our brains. You almost felt like you'd missed something even though you'd just SEEN it—only because you hadn't heard Harry call it.

So after that game, I headed for the clubhouse. And as I've been known to do on days I have time to write, I spent every moment in that clubhouse that I could, looking for one more quote or one more great scene to add to the texture of the story. Little did I know what a great scene was about to present itself.

Schmitty and his teammates did all the interviews there were to be done. They'd gotten dressed. The bus to the hotel was waiting. It was time to go—except it wasn't. Not quite yet. Into that clubhouse walked Harry and the broadcast crew, and they'd brought with them a tape of the home run call.

Well, life in that clubhouse came to just about a complete stop. Everybody gathered around the tape recorder—me included—just to listen to Harry Kalas call a home run he'd been born to call: Mike Schmidt's 500th homer.

They listened to that call, one of Harry's greatest ever. And they screamed so loudly, it's amazing the walls of the stadium didn't crumble. But that wasn't end of it. They needed to hear that call again. And again. And again.

I remember thinking, How amazing is this? It's almost like, even for them—even for the players—this didn't really feel like it happened until they'd heard Harry call it. And that's when I realized: Harry Kalas wasn't just the soundtrack of our lives. He was the soundtrack of their lives, too.

—**Jayson Stark**, ESPN, author of *Worth the Wait*,
about the 2008 Phillies

> When Philadelphia sportswriters resort to a rarely used gear—unconditional praise—you know he was someone special.

Harry Kalas would be humbled by the reaction to his passing. They boo everything that walks in Philadelphia, including Santa Claus, but when the voice of the Phillies died, shock prevailed, followed by sorrow.

Even crabby journalists opened up their shirts and let their hearts fall out, hailing Kalas as a giant in the business with no apparent sense of hubris. When Philadelphia sportswriters resort to a rarely used gear—unconditional praise—you know he was someone special.

The Phillies lost their voice, and the fans lost their friend. Yet it is comforting to know that such relationships still exist in a hurried, high-tech world where play-by-play accounts of a game are available on computers and pitch-by-pitch on cell phones.

You don't need the sports page to find a box score, and you don't need a broadcaster to explain how it happened as it happens. Still, your announcer for your ballclub can be a family member without pedigree, joining us to provide daily relief, entertainment and stability.

Baseball announcers represent a soundtrack for our lives, not sound bites for our short attention spans. Kalas' passion confirmed he would rather be no place but the ballpark. One can only hope baseball does not become so corporate and controlling that there is no room for distinctive individuals to rent to us, summer after summer. Back in the stone ages, when the World Series meant afternoon games best monitored by strategically hidden radios that schoolteachers could not detect, it didn't matter if the man on the scene had a face made for radio.

Kalas was the Phillies, but in an age of homogenized presentation and shared content, the fear is that his ilk will yield to a new breed seeking safety in sameness. We don't need clowns or clones. There are enough of both in other industries.

With athletes less approachable and tickets less affordable than ever, we want broadcasters with soul. A one-way conversation is fine if the messenger isn't a sound-alike or think-alike. Kalas was the son of a minister with the voice of God, but that's not why he bonded with fans. We listened because he did it his way and never had a bad day until his last one.

—**Bob Verdi**, journalist, Chicago

Once on a spring-training trip to the Dominican Republic we rented a car in Santo Domingo for a journey across the country for an exhibition game against the St. Louis Cardinals. The car was tired and really didn't want to run.

Harry decided it needed oil. I have a picture on my wall at home of Kalas pouring motor oil into the engine of the car, something he'd never done before.

"Do you really think that's going to help?" Ashburn asked.

"Positively," said Kalas. "All this baby needs is some oil. Trust me."

"It's hot. It really needs water, not oil," said Whitey.

"You can't mix water and oil, Whitey," Harry said.

We made it to the game, but en route back we stopped at a roadside stand. As we pulled up some natives with guns came down from the hills.

"Don't worry about a thing, boys," Ashburn said, reaching into a canvas bag. "I'll take care of them." He pulled out a knife hardly big enough to peel a potato.

Kalas laughed and pushed on the gas, a cloud of dust trailing behind.

Harry and I often rented a car for the trip between Los Angeles and San Diego, and whenever possible stopped at the famed resort La Costa for a round of golf.

Once after spending a night at La Costa, Harry and I were up early for a round of golf and a gentleman asked if he could join us. Whitey had gone on to San Diego.

Turns out this man was an officer at Riviera Country Club in Los Angeles and invited us to play there whenever we could.

We took him up on it many times, and one day when we finished a round Dean Martin was sitting in a golf cart, getting ready to play.

We chatted with him for several moments and en route back to the hotel Harry was singing some of Dean's favorite songs.

—**Hal Bodley**, baseball editor and columnist
for 25 years at *USA Today*

Chapter Five

HARRYPALOOZA

Randy Duncan
John Bouma
Richard Whittington
Gib Drendel
John Miley
Steve Sabol
Kent Tekulve

Too Much Ain't Enough

RANDY DUNCAN IS A LAWYER. WHY DID YOU THINK HE WAS A STOCKBROKER? "I HEARD HE HANDLED JUNK BLONDES!"

Randy Duncan

Randy Duncan was Harry Kalas' favorite fellow student and classmate at the University of Iowa. Now a very successful lawyer in Des Moines, the All-American quarterback recently mused about his college days.

He was second in the Heisman voting and was the first overall choice in the 1959 NFL draft. He spurned the Green Bay Packers with their rookie coach, Vince Lombardi, and signed with the CFL (Canadian Football League) for bigger dollars. Forest Evashevski called Duncan the most improved, most pleasant surprise of all his Iowa players. Duncan was picked College Player of the Year by three organizations in 1958, but many older randy Iowans remember him for an incident at the end of his sophomore season.

When I was a sophomore, there was a reporter—I don't know where he was from—calling up all the ballplayers. "What do you want for New Year's Day when you go to California for the Rose Bowl?" All of them were saying, "A victory over Oregon State." I wanted a victory over Oregon State, but I said, "Hey, I want a date with Jayne Mansfield."

Somebody in the Los Angeles area picked it up off an Iowa story, and they must have gotten in touch with her before the Big Ten banquet they had every year. The banquet was in Los Angeles, and Bob Hope was the emcee. I remember Bob Hope said, "The first time I heard the name Forest Evashevski, I thought it was a park in Russia."

There we are at the banquet, and all of a sudden Hope introduces Jayne Mansfield. She said, "I want to see one of the Iowa football players, and his name is Randy Duncan." Oh man, I got right up there. I grabbed her and gave her a great big smooch. It was great! She was really put together. There's a picture somewhere. I had both hands on both her buns. All my teammates are yelling at me—I became a hero overnight to my teammates. The place was going wild. She didn't say anything, just went along with the gag.

When we got back to the frat house in Iowa City, Harry Kalas thought that was the greatest accomplishment of mankind. He talked about it for months. I've talked about it for years.

I first met Harry at the University of Iowa, where he just a regular guy. In fact, I didn't realize until recently that Harry was as big of a deal as he turned out to be. I knew he did the Phillies games and the work with the NFL, but he had a national following that I didn't imagine.

At Iowa, we called him the "White Rat," because he had really white hair. When he'd go swimming, you'd see his pink scalp. For some reason that really stands out. At the same time, he always called me "ornery," but to this day I can't tell you why.

The most memorable story to me about Harry during school is how he was always broke. He would write checks for 50 cents. If he needed some gas, he'd write a check for 50 cents. When I'd ask him about it or give him a hard time, he'd say, "That's all I have in my account." That was his answer every time. Then, once a month he would get money from his dad and he could write checks for more than 50 cents. He was just busted all of the time, but writing those checks didn't bother him, though.

He was a fun-loving guy who had a basically normal background, but an abnormal voice. His dad was a minister and Harry was the proverbial minister's son. He liked to drink beer and have fun. He was a typical college guy. In Iowa City, we had a beer called Ace beer. It was horrible, but Kalas was always first in line getting it. Even back then, 10 cents for a bottle of beer was dirt cheap. But it tasted like a 10-cent beer. That's what we bought.

> He had a normal background but an abnormal voice.

Of course, he was on the campus radio station, WSUI, and I played football, so I was always asking him for more air time. [Editor's note: In an interview with writer Ron Maly, Kalas is quoted as saying of Duncan: "In fact, he helped me in a project I had to do in one of my television courses. I had some Hawk-eye game film, and Randy was kind enough to come over to the studio and dissect the plays for me. I'd say, 'OK, Randy, it's third down-and-eight. What would you do here?' "He'd say what they might do on that play. I got an A on the project, thanks to Randy Duncan."] The story isn't as familiar to Duncan.

I do remember him interviewing me for something, but I hadn't heard the part about the A. That could be apocryphal, but it sure makes for a better story.

You know, people go through your life that you forget about. Kalas was the kind of guy who you never forgot. With the exception of writing each other every once in a while, we didn't really stay in touch. With that voice that he had, I knew he'd be successful but I never thought he'd have the national reputation that he gained. He had a normal background but an abnormal voice.

We had a very 1950s-type relationship. I basically remember just drinking beer and talking. We didn't worry about anything. We went to school, drank beer and had fun. Ultimately, we just wanted to succeed in life. I'd like to think we accomplished that.

BEER WAS THE REASON
THEY GOT UP EVERY AFTERNOON

John Bouma

John Bouma is a senior partner in one of the most prestigious law firms in America— Snell & Wilmer in Phoenix. A native of Pocahontas, Iowa, he fondly recalls his old frat-house pal Harry Kalas.

Harry, who was nicknamed the "White Rat" because of his light hair, was a fraternity brother of mine at the Phi Delta house at the University of Iowa in the 1950s. We quickly became good friends. I graduated in 1958, so he was a year behind me. He was interested in being a broadcaster, but I don't recall his career as a broadcaster being spectacular at Iowa. I know he broadcast some games, but he also worked at the U of I radio station. He'd get up in the morning and go down there . . . until he got fired because he wasn't very good about getting up in the morning. In my memory that didn't last very long. Harry just took things in stride.

He really liked baseball and always talked about Harmon Killebrew, whom he thought was the hottest thing going in those days.

In those days, you had to either be in the ROTC or the National Guard, because otherwise you'd get drafted. I was in the ROTC and Harry wasn't. However, he kept screwing around and didn't do it. His father was a minister and president of Westmar College in Le Mars, Iowa, so Harry decided to go back home and join the National Guard right after school. The day that school ended in his senior year, he got his draft notice at our fraternity house. Of course, it turned out OK for him, though, because the next thing I knew, he was walking around Hawaii with a tape recorder, interviewing people. Harry had a way of coming up with things pretty well. That worked for him and got him some of the experience to get into broadcasting. As far as I know, he never got sent to any combat, so I don't think getting drafted hurt him at all. I had not heard the story until recently about him meeting Buddy Blattner in a bar over there, but it doesn't surprise me that things started for him in a bar.

We used to go to the Airliner, the popular bar in Iowa City. About six or seven times, we'd decide at the spur of the moment to take off when the bar closed at 1 a.m., drive all night to Chicago and catch a baseball game. We'd grab a couple of six-packs and get to town around dawn. If we got there early enough, we'd try to find a place to sleep. One time I remember, we were going to a White Sox game. We had been drinking our six-packs, and then we were drinking at Comiskey Park. The game seemed to go about 17 innings, although it was probably only about 12, and we fell asleep during the middle of the game. We woke up, though, before the end and started drinking beer again.

They used to have giveaways at the stadium, and you won if you had something attached to the bottom of your seat. On a different trip to a White Sox game, Harry won a bunch of pickles.

My girlfriend at the time, who's now my wife, was named Bonnie Lane. Harry, who was always into sports, used to call her "Night Train," after the Detroit Lions famous Dick "Night Train" Lane. She was from Aurora, Illinois, which was between Iowa City and Chicago. I remember we stopped there on one trip and she gave us some homemade fried chicken to take with us. Harry didn't like it so he gave it to the parking lot attendant.

Harry was originally from Naperville, Illinois. On our way back to Iowa after one of those trips to Chicago, we decided to go to Naperville and see if we could find some of his friends. In those days, none of us had any money. Harry and I, and a few of his friends, were trying to figure out what to eat. One of the guys remembered there was a Polish wedding in a town nearby. So, four or five of us went to this Polish wedding reception. We didn't know anybody, but we kept eating the food and drinking their beer, and we'd comment to people about how beautiful the bride was. It was probably obvious that we didn't belong because we were wearing our Bermuda shorts and T-shirts, but the people were wonderful to us; very welcoming. In this day and age you'd get thrown out for something like that. I guess you can say we were the original Wedding Crashers long before the movie.

At the University of Iowa at the time, there was a rule against alcohol on campus. Another fraternity brother and I sold beer in our room after the Airliner closed at night. We'd buy it at the store and then sell it for a slight profit. The only problem was that a lot of those guys wanted to hang out in our room and talk. One of our best customers was Harry, and he'd hang out like everyone else. It was probably during one of those nights when Harry and I cooked up an idea to go to Colorado for a summer.

We went to Colorado Springs in the summer of 1956 because we had a friend who told us he had gotten us jobs as waiters at the tavern at the famous Broadmoor Hotel. My dad was unenthusiastic about that, but I talked him out of our car, which was very nice. It was a Buick special, one of the first hardtops. It was yellow with a dark gray top. So, we drove out there. The same time, the lady I'd been dating some, who's now my wife, and two or three of her sorority sisters drove out there, too.

When Harry and I showed up at the Broadmoor, they hadn't even heard of us! There weren't jobs waiting for us and they sent us away. Suddenly we were in Colorado and didn't have any money. We went to the old Antlers Hotel and got signed on as waiters for banquets. The first thing we had to do was serve breakfast at a banquet. We didn't know anything about serving tables. How hard could it be? Harry was such a nice guy that when he went back to get the food for his table, he wouldn't push his way through with the other waiters. Guys would come in, grab their food and serve their tables. As a result, the people at Harry's tables got honked off and we both got fired. We lasted about a day doing that. Then, we started looking around for another job, and we went over to Cripple Creek. Here we are, two college guys with our butch haircuts and button-down shirts, driving up to a construction site and asking if they were hiring. We didn't have a lot of success. But we had a good time. We were so short on money that we had a discussion about whether to buy food or just get beer and eat popcorn. We decided on the latter.

We couldn't find a job at Cripple Creek or anywhere else, so we finally persuaded them at the golf course at the Broadmoor to let us work there. We were the lowest form of employee they had there. We were among the alcoholics and crowd of misfits. But there we were. Besides spreading fertilizer and mowing the grass, they had us digging the cart paths, which were new in those days. We dug those for a while.

Again, we weren't making any money, so we didn't have a way to entertain ourselves. One of the things we'd do is go over to the Broadmoor, get some bread out of the back and go feed the ducks. Or, we'd go party at the Garden of the Gods.

Harry was slightly built in those days. Do you remember those great big ice machines where you'd put in your money and the ice would come down a chute? When we needed ice, Harry was small enough to crawl up in one of those and grab a bag of ice. While we were in Colorado Springs, we stayed at the Phi Delta house. That's how we survived.

As I mentioned, I dated my wife out there. One night, around the Fourth of July, I was going out with her, and she was going to drive her car. Harry wanted to take my car. He was driving along and saw a girl in some short shorts. He kept staring and staring, until he drove that nice car into a parked semi. The next day, Harry and I went into a bar and we were watching a baseball game. I said, "Well, it's time to call my dad and tell him about the accident." I think it's the only time I ever hung up on my father. It didn't help that I was in Colorado, where he didn't want me in the first place, in the Buick, and Harry was the one who wrecked it. That wasn't good. Harry and I had an interesting conversation that night, though. He was telling me about his father being a minister and about his brother who had done well in ministry, but Harry talked about how he was always the black sheep of the family. He was depressed about all of that. It was a conversation that I'll never forget.

Harry and I continued to work at the golf course at the Broadmoor, until we were fired. This time it wasn't necessarily our fault. The **AIR FORCE ACADEMY*** had just started, and Frederick Maytag of Maytag Appliances was a big member of the Broadmoor Country Club. He donated some of the land—or had been involved somehow—in getting the golf course started for the Air Force Academy. The Air Force Academy had some big-time athletes coming in to play basketball, but they didn't qualify academically. So, the Air Force Academy was going to stash them at Pueblo Community College so they could get qualified. Well, Maytag had them fire us and hire those guys. At least that's what I've heard. I found another job driving a truck hauling pipe for a bridge supply outfit. Harry signed on as a waiter somewhere. Harry's problem was the gay guys always hitting on him. Remember, he was slightly built. The problem was that he always thought he could tell which guys were hitting on him or he could be friends with. He'd come home from a movie, thinking he was going with a guy who wanted to be friends, but the guy would hit on him during the movie. It was pretty funny at the time.

Today, thinking about the Broadmoor is interesting on a personal note. Harry and I couldn't even get in the door at the Broadmoor. We were dirt. Now, for our law firm, I chair a couple conferences there, and we get the nicest suites. I've laughed with the people at the Broadmoor about that summer with Harry.

As is the case with many people, Harry and I stayed in touch better in the years following school than later in life. The last time I actually saw Harry was several years ago when Notre Dame was

*Bill Parcells was head coach at the **AIR FORCE ACADEMY** in 1978. His record was 3-8.

playing in the Fiesta Bowl. Harry was out there doing the game on radio, and he came by afterwards for a party we were having. We sat around the bar and talked for a few hours. It was a great conversation.

A few years after that, I was being honored in Philadelphia, and for some reason our group was at the offices of the Inquirer. On the newspaper rack were all of these pages honoring Harry for his induction into the Baseball Hall of Fame that day. I saw it and started laughing, telling the folks there that Harry was a good friend of mine, and I'd like to talk to him. After much asking and much persuasion, they gave me his phone number. I called him that night. I said, "Harry, this is John Bouma." "Boomer!" he responded. "How's 'Night Train?'" That was the first thing he said to me. Any time we talked, it was as if we'd stayed in constant contact, even though it might've been seven or eight years. That was the last time I talked to him.

What a guy!

Harry Kalas (L) is congratulated by Hall of Famer Robin Roberts following the Baseball Hall of Fame induction ceremony, July 28, 2002. Photo by Charles Fox.

TIME WELL WASTED

Richard Whittington

Richard Whittington of Cupertino, California, hasn't seen or talked to Harry Kalas in over 40 years. But he vividly remembers working with Kalas on a summer construction job in July and August 1958—just prior to their senior year at the University of Iowa. Whittington, a native of Hawarden, Iowa, is retired after many years in construction machinery sales.

We were working doing finishing concrete jobs—streets, curbs and gutters—in Carroll, Iowa. I had never met Harry before this. Western Construction was the parent company doing streets in my hometown of Hawarden. I signed on during the summer when I was in college. When we completed the work there, they invited some of us who they considered to be pretty good workers to move with them to Carroll, Iowa. While there, I stayed in a rooming house for $35 a month. Harry lived somewhere else, maybe with his folks in Le Mars, Iowa where his dad was president of a college

Harry arrived on the scene and was working on our crew paving streets. I became a finisher and Harry did mostly light finishing work. Harry and I were paid $1.38 an hour, with no overtime, and we worked sun-up to dark, light to light, six days a week. Sometimes, we may have gotten off early on Saturday.

We worked many, many hours in hot summer weather. Harry and I worked closely together. Our crew, except for the two of us, was mostly minorities—Indians and blacks from Sioux City. We had a great crew working together, and they liked us and would joke with Harry all the time. We didn't have much time off, but Harry and I did manage to get to the local ballroom and drink some beer and do some dancing. Harry was a good-looking guy and was popular when we got to go to the ballroom.

When Harry quit, he said he was going down to Iowa City and would stop back and spend a day or so with us. He did come back a few weeks later and the crew was all happy to see him.

Harry was hardworking, well liked in his work. In his own way, he was easygoing—almost laid back, but very much there. He was outgoing and very open-minded. In those days, blacks and Indians were definitely considered lower minorities, and Harry and I got looked down on at times because we had such great rapport with them and became good friends with them. Some of the other white guys wouldn't have much to do with us. We liked them because we considered them just another person, and that's all there was to it. . . .

A few years ago I was going back to Milwaukee on business and the plane was being de-iced. I had a radio with me and was listening to it. Harry was broadcasting a ball game. I said, "I know that voice!" On the radio, they don't say their names often so I listened for a while and finally he said, "This is Harry Kalas and so-and-so in the booth . . ." About that time, the plane took off and I couldn't hear him anymore. It had been over 40 years since I had heard that voice. . . .

I saw one of those Internet things telling you how to locate your friends, so I sent his name in. I got an answer with information on it, but I never did follow up because I was afraid it was not the same Harry Kalas. Or, if it was, that he might think I was just looking for free tickets to a game. I didn't want it to be like that.

Harry was just like the rest of the guys. We would go out at night sometimes and get some drinks. All of us smoked at that time. Harry called everybody "little brother." He called me "little Richard." His personality was such that you just loved being around him. I would have loved to have been in contact with him later on because I always idolized him. Where have the years gone? It all seems like 12 minutes ago.

WHEN I WENT TO HIGH SCHOOL WITH HARRY, THE WORLD WAS DIFFERENT. FOR ONE THING IT WAS FLAT.

Gib Drendel

Gib Drendel still lives in his hometown of Naperville, Illinois, where he was a high school classmate of Harry Kalas. They were college classmates until Kalas was requested to take his studies and antics elsewhere. Drendel is a family law attorney in Batavia, Illinois.

Harry's dad was a minister and taught at North Central seminary in the area. Later, his father was a bishop and was president of Westmar College in Iowa.

In high school, our class was not large so Harry and I ran around together a lot. Harry was short—5'4"—and, while he loved sports, he was not able to really compete. He played linebacker a little bit, but he was too little. As an adult, Harry was at least six feet, maybe more.

Harry asked my now-wife, Carol, for a date, and they were going to go to a movie drive-in theater. Her mother cautioned her that he was a minister's son and they can sometimes be pretty difficult, so she warned her to be extra careful. They went to the drive-in. Carol, when she got home, said, "He was no problem at all. He sat there all night practicing baseball announcing."

Harry was absolutely driven to do that. He also loved to play cards. He loved to smoke. He liked his beer. He was a minister's kid—a very typical one.

When he was doing the play-by-play back then, we thought he sounded pretty good, but we never thought he had a future doing that. Once he drew our attention by doing it, he kept doing it. It always triggered a response and joshing and kept the kids talking about it. But, we didn't think he was serious. We knew he loved baseball . . . we all did. It was just that he liked to do that. We called him "Potsy." To us, we thought it meant "small."

He didn't date much in high school. He ran around with the guys. I went to Cornell College in Mount Vernon, Iowa, along with Harry. It was a Methodist school and was a state school with curfews for women to be in their dorms. That didn't quite suit Harry's personality at that time. There's no doubt that Harry was found on the fire escape at the girls' dorm after hours. He got a three-week suspension about mid-freshman year.

Then, finals week, Harry and another fellow were bored and were shooting off firecrackers in a metal wastebasket, which caught the attention of the proctor. That was enough. They invited him not to come back. That's how he ended up down at the University of Iowa. After he got down there, I didn't see Harry much.

But while at Cornell, Harry took a speech course from a blind speech professor, Dr. Walter Stroemer. Harry always said, "Once I began to speak in class, Dr. Stroemer said, 'You have a voice and should be on the radio.'" So, Harry had that voice that early. He practiced that voice very hard. He had as a goal—and he really talked about it in high school—that he would be a baseball announcer.

During our first year at Cornell, I became a real student, and he was still quite a socializer so our paths differed a little bit. We ran with different kids that year in college.

From time to time, we would see him when he came to Chicago to broadcast games. The last time I saw him was last August. We had a class reunion. We had scheduled the reunion so that if he wanted to or could come, he'd be in town . . . and he did come. As it turned out, it was a sort-of farewell. We scheduled it when the Phillies were in town because he generally couldn't come. He came out after the Friday game. He didn't look well to me and, apparently, he wasn't. That would have been our 54th class reunion. We'd had such a good 50th reunion in 2004.

Many people didn't come and wished they had, so we decided the class of 1954 could have a 54th reunion. It was one of those things. It was fine, and we had a lot of fun. We had 110 people in our class and all the people who came to the reunion knew what Harry was doing and that he was in the Hall of Fame.

At the reunion, I was a little sobered by the fact that he didn't look well. He had a pallor and wasn't robust. But, given our age, a number of people were that way. The last time I'd seen him, he was much more like the old Harry. Harry led us in "High Hopes." He had stopped drinking and was drinking a soft drink. We recounted old stories—a typical reunion scene. We were at a private home on Friday. On Saturday we had another event, but Harry was calling a game at Wrigley so he could not attend that.

Harry was the ringleader of a lot of things. He drove the pastor's car on a lot of these evenings when we did things we shouldn't have done.

We had an incident when some of the guys from our class placed some kind of a smelly cheese in the boys' restroom. We had radiators in those days and we put this cheese in there. Of course, it stunk up the hall. The baseball and assistant football coach's room was near there. Coach gathered everyone who was anywhere near, or who was on that floor, and lined us up. He asked us who did it. Fess up. Nobody told. What he then did, he made us hold our hands out, and he went along and smelled hands. He found the guys who put the cheese in there. Harry was one of those guys. That is the kind of thing Harry would always have been in the middle of.

I write family history books so I have a pretty good sense of history and time, but I couldn't answer Harry's question at the reunion, "Where has all the time gone?" A bunch of our group married one another, and there wasn't one divorce in the bunch! It was that kind of a place. It was that kind of a time.

INSTANT NOSTALGIA?
JUST ADD TAPES AND YEARN

John Miley

John Miley, 78, is the biggest sports fan in Evansville, Indiana, and he can prove it. Miley has thousands of tapes of games and interviews from thousands of sports announcers going back to 1947. He started with a wire recorder, went to reel-to-reel, then cassettes and now CDs. Miley has over 500 Harry Kalas tapes.

When I started out, I was doing it just for myself, thinking that when I retire—which I now believe is never going to happen—I would have something to do because I love to listen to sporting events. Bill Stern was my favorite announcer in the past.

This collection has kept me "young." My wife takes 80,000 pills a day, and I take one pill. I told her I would probably die before her of a heart attack. You just never know when you're going to go. I'm a Cardinal fan, so I started by taping some of the Cardinal games. I didn't realize I would start a collection until around 1962. So, from '47 to '62, it was just here, there and everywhere. I might have saved something on my wire recorder or reel but then again I might have erased over it. I finally realized I should save some of the stuff I had.

In 1962 I decided I'd try to get every baseball team on tape once during each season. I only save highlights. I had a tremendous article written about me in late December 1977, in *Sporting News*. At the end of it, I said, "I have two or three people around the nation taping for me—one in Dallas, one in North Carolina and others in case I needed something in those areas." There wasn't such a thing as the Internet in those days. At the end of the deal, the writer said, "If you want to join John Miley's tape network, contact him at 441 Scenic Drive, Evansville, Indiana, 47715. I got letters from Europe. I got a letter from a 12-year-old kid in Boston who said, "I'd be glad to help you out." I didn't impose upon him, but I really developed one tremendous tape network . . . and I wasn't even trying to do that.

Take the Cal-Stanford game of 1982. I had a guy at Travis Air Force Base outside of San Francisco I had met through the article. He started taping the California college and pro teams. He knew how much I liked the Cal-Stanford game, but I didn't think that game would have any interest that year of 1982 so I didn't ask him to tape it. He called me that evening at six o'clock and asked, "Did you hear what happened in the Cal-Stanford game?" He started telling me the story. I said, "Halt. I don't want to know. It sounds like something great happened, and I know I didn't ask you to tape it so I don't want to know about it." This made me sick. He said, "John, I taped it on both the Stanford and the California network." I said, "Wrap that stuff up and insure it for a million dollars and send it on Monday." So, I have that game on both networks, complete. That's how things have happened.

I ran into Harry Kalas when the Astros got him in 1965. I thought this guy had some talent. He really sounded good to me. I am very critical of announcers, both positive and negative. There are a number of negative announcers, including Curt Smith's 100 list. As far as I'm concerned, he's got a bunch of negatives on there, but he puts his list out in a different way than I would. We're all different so I'm certainly not complaining with him. I enjoyed listening to Kalas on that network.

Then, he went to Philadelphia in 1971 where Byrum Saam was the play-by-play guy. I loved Byrum—he was absolutely sensational. He was so good he was selected for at least one, and probably several, World Series. You don't get selected for the World Series back in those days unless you were good. I just loved the way he delivered. He and Harry Kalas made a heck of a team of play-by-play announcers.

Bill Campbell is a great announcer. Philadelphia has had a number of great announcers. I have Bill Campbell doing the fourth quarter of the Wilt Chamberlain game where he got 100 points.

I have everything on the computer. I've got 533 things on my computer with Harry Kalas. My first thing is on 4/8/65, Harry Kalas interviews Joe DiMaggio. The next thing is the Houston Astros beating the Yankees in an exhibition game, where Mantle hit the first home run in the Astrodome. Harry, Elston and Loel Passe are doing that game. The next game I've got him with Gene Elston on May 31, 1965.

Harry Kalas was as good in football as he was in baseball. I love his football broadcasts. I have a number of them.

When I first started listening to Harry, most all of the announcers in those days were good. I had my favorite announcers, but I didn't have my non-favorite announcers.

Because I wasn't able to get Houston when Harry Kalas came on with them, and I wasn't that interested in the Philadelphia Phillies, I didn't listen to that much of him. The main thing I can say is what I was able to collect most of his best stuff after 1977. I thought his call of Mike Schmidt's 500th home run was one of the great calls of all time.

I've got these five plaques of famous sports calls. They have a button at the front, and when you push it, you get the call. One of the five is Kalas' call on Schmidt. This company produced these pictures where you can punch the little baseball in the middle of the picture and get the highlight of each event. Those did not sell very well, so they went out of business. I have these five on my wall. I thought it was a brilliant idea, but they sold for $75 apiece and I guess people were just not willing to pay that amount of money. They are beautiful.

Harry Kalas was no John Facenda—there's only one. But, to replace him with Harry Kalas was a tremendous honor. It's like replacing Harry Caray with somebody or Jack Brickhouse or whatever . . . or replacing Harry Kalas.

IF YOU RUN NFL FILMS BACKWARDS, IT LOOKS LIKE THE PLAYERS ARE HELPING EACH OTHER UP AND SHOWING THEM ON THEIR WAY

Steve Sabol

NFL Films were established in 1964, when Ed Sabol, Steve's father, convinced then-NFL Commissioner Pete Rozelle that the league needed a motion picture company to record its history. NFL Films has mushroomed well beyond the role of mere historian.

Harry Kalas provided the narration for many of this organization's productions, beginning in 1975. He shared those duties at first with another legendary voice, that of Philadelphia newsman John Facenda, and then became NFL Films' primary narrator after Facenda's death in 1984—a position Harry held all the way through the 2008 season. Sabol spoke at Kalas' memorial service, noting that in addition to the two great sounds Walt Whitman once wrote about—that of the wind and the sea—there was a third: "Harry Kalas, rising to the roar of the crowd."

To me, Harry is a relic of another era, where people held one job for years. You look at the great broadcasters today—John Madden, Bob Costas—they move around from job to job, network to network. Harry was the last of his breed, because he cared enough to stick around. He loved his job, and he didn't want to go anyplace else. People don't do that anymore. He was modest, he was approachable, he was unassuming and the more I got to know him, he grew into this legend. And he was a legend without acting like one. It's sad to realize that you've lost someone you've been attached to, for so long. Then you realize you've lost something more than just a person; you've lost an attachment to something that will never, ever be repaired or replicated. And I mean Harry's talent.

When we started with Facenda, John had that voice which made it seem like he was reading a script as if it was carved on stone tablets. Facenda was a unique voice and a unique talent, but I began to realize that he couldn't do all of our films. There were epic films, there were films of the championships, but when we were doing a highlight film of a team that won four games, Facenda was not the right voice. It was like hunting butterflies with a sledgehammer—it just didn't work. And we needed a voice that was more contemporary, and a voice that still had a feeling for the weight and tone of words. I said at Harry's funeral, Facenda was the voice of God; Harry was the voice of the people. But he had a sincerity, a contemporary feeling to his voice, an immediacy and an energy. The problem was, when I wanted to hire him, the people here said, "Well, he's a baseball guy. Why do you want that?" I said, "I'm looking at broader horizons here. He's known to all of us, here in Philadelphia as the voice of the Phillies. But in Denver, in **SEATTLE***, in Dallas, they don't know Harry Kalas, and we can start to use him for football. He can be known locally as the voice of the Phillies, but nationally, if this works out, he'll be the voice of NFL Films."

The first couple times we used him, there was always that feeling: Well, is he the right guy? But I stuck with him, and the more films he narrated, the teams decided they liked him, and the fans nationally responded to him. Harry had a talent that he could turn a phrase with the proper emphasis on the key words. There's not a lot of play-by-play men that have a voice that can cut through music, and still have the drama to it. Most play-by-play men are

---

*During the **SEATTLE** Mariners' first year in 1977, the distance to the fences was measured in fathoms. A fathom is 6 feet. For instance, whereas one park might have a sign that denotes 360 feet, the Kingdome sign would have the number 60 . . .

used because of their facility and their spontaneous usage of the English language, and their knowledge of the sport. Harry had all of that, but also he was born a gift of, as my father used to say, great tonsils. He had a great voice, and he was the perfect counterbalance to Facenda. He could read a script, he could look at it and didn't need to rehearse it. His delivery was always seamless, flawless; he never stumbled over any words. He was a great reader, and that's really what he did for us, as opposed to what he did for baseball.

He could have a hangover, he could be suffering from a cold, he could have a sore throat—whatever it was his delivery was still crisp. That's the sign of a real pro: They can perform no matter what. I remember when Harry was going through his divorce from his first wife, Jasmine, and how awful that was—how distraught he was. But when we went on air and they tapped him on the shoulder, he was a pro. In spite of all the Parliament cigarettes and the Tanqueray and tonics, Harry's voice remained as resonant as Yo-Yo Ma's cello. He had a tone. I'm not saying Harry was an alcoholic, but Harry took every at-bat, and he played every inning.

He was certainly a constant in my life, as a friend, a broadcaster, a narrator. He's someone who will be succeeded but never replaced. We've already had 47 people send in audition tapes to replace him. A lot of them are already making the same mistake hopefuls did when Facenda passed away. We had 75 different people—everyone from Ed McMahon to Robert Stack to Burl Ives, people that wanted to do it. But everybody imitated Facenda. We realized you can't replace a Sinatra or an Elvis; you've got to go in a different direction. What we've noticed in the tapes we've got now is that people are trying to imitate Harry. We can't do that. We've got to find someone else who is his own voice, his own talent, and start from scratch.

You just listen to resonance in the voices of potential successors. You listen to their ability to tell a story, to turn a phrase. And if they get past that, you send them another script, and then we put music to it, and we see how much music their voice can play under, or play above. We have a very hot mix. We spend hundreds of thousands of dollars on music. We use the Philadelphia Orchestra musicians. We have the most honored documentary composer on television in Dave Robidoux, so the music is very, very important. In some cases the sound is more important than the script or narration. We have to find a narrator whose voice has the resonance to handle a full 70-piece orchestra behind him. Facenda was like that, and Harry was good at that, too.

Harry was a quicker read and knew the game better than John did. Sometimes you had to explain to John. The other thing was, John never read the picture, because he used to feel rushed. Harry read the picture, so there was a timing element. With John, we had a good feeling of his cadence, and then he would just get in the recording booth and just read the script, without ever seeing the picture. Harry did everything the other way. Harry read to the picture. He would be looking at a little monitor and also reading at the same time. It made it a little more complicated than the way John did it.

Our first sponsor was Red Devil Caulking. Our show, *Inside the NFL*, was on late Saturday night, then syndicated early Sunday morning. They were what you would call now our presenting sponsor, but there wasn't that terminology then. But they were paying the most money. It was one of those products where you could fix a leaky roof or a drafty basement with it, or it could repair a tire. And they wanted all of that information in the open, and it was like 175 words. You had to get it on in 20 seconds. I said, "There is no way humanly possible that this can be read in 20 seconds." And they said, "Well, it's important, because our product's so unique. You've got to get all this information in." Not only did Harry get it right, he did it in one take. That became one of the legendary moments in narration in NFL Films history—Harry Kalas and Red Devil Caulking. Not one stumble. Every word came out clear. Everything was crisp. He enunciated everything, and it was like the Evelyn Wood of narration. When that happened, there were about six or seven of us in the studio, and he got a standing ovation. No one could believe it. That became part of the Kalas legend. Any time we wanted Harry to do something quicker, instead of Facenda saying, "fortunato," we'd always say, "Red Devil it, Harry." And he knew what that meant—that that meant he'd have to pick up the pace.

He was good at football play-by-play, but Harry made more money from the commercials that ensued after the first 10 or 15 years with us. Then he became the voice of NFL Films, and he was the voice of Coors, and he was the voice of Campbell Soup, and he did GM Trucks. I remember sitting in an airport with Harry, and we were having a few drinks. The GM Truck commercial came up, and we watched it. Harry just turned around to me, and he took his arm and he went, "Cha-ching." That was where the money was. We always used to kid that he made more money from those commercials than he ever did from us.

[The following is the author's favorite sports story and he includes it in every Steve Sabol interview.]

I can't believe you remembered the story of the "Fearless Tot from Possum Trot." What happened was I was raised in a suburb of Philadelphia called Villanova, Pennsylvania. I had great grades in prep school but I had lousy SAT scores so I ended up going to school in Colorado Springs at a college called Colorado College. I wanted to play football out there, so one of the first things I did was change my hometown from Villanova to Coaltown Township, Pennsylvania. It was a nonexistent town but had the ring of solid football to it. Everybody knows that western Pennsylvania is where the football studs come from. I'd never seen a coal mine but if coaches thought I had been rubbing shoulders with guys like Mike Ditka and Leon Hart, they'd have to start thinking. I carried it off all freshman year and nobody caught on. Guys would come up and ask me why I hadn't gotten a big scholarship from Notre Dame or Ohio State or someplace, and I'd just say, "Aw, I was just third string."

But I didn't play much freshman year so I knew I'd have to do something to impress the coaches. So when I came back for sophomore year, I told everyone that I was from Possum Trot, Mississippi, 'cause you can't ignore anyone from a place called

Possum Trot. Then I knew I had to change my name. I had an honorable name but it didn't have the ring of greatness. I wanted something real lethal like "Sudden Death." that fit my initials, too—Steven Douglas Sabol became Steve "Sudden Death" Sabol. Then in the program for the very first game, we had "Sudden Death" Sabol listed by that name. Also I bought an ad in the program that said, "Coach Jerry Carle wishes "Sudden Death" Sabol a successful season." Everybody thought the coach put the ad in there, but I paid for the ad myself. Coach Carle was a regular Bear Bryant: he never smiled. The last thing he'd do would be wish me a successful season, but a lot of people took it seriously. I thought it was all pretty funny. But the coach didn't have any scholarships to give so he couldn't run off any players like me.

Unfortunately I only weighed one hundred and seventy pounds, so the nickname "Sudden Death" just didn't seem to go with my build. Nevertheless, in the final program of the season, I ran an ad that said "Coach Jerry Carle congratulates "Sudden Death" Sabol on a fantastic season."

So before my junior year, I added forty pounds—I really bulked up. Then I started sending out press agent stuff to both the local and the Denver papers. One ad told everyone "The Possum Trot Chamber of Commerce extends its wishes for a successful season to its favorite son, 'Sudden Death' Sabol." Another advertisement included a picture of me in a football uniform at about the age of ten in Philadelphia where I played on a Midget League team, called the Little Quakers. Then came a hundred T-shirts made up with the drawing of a possum and the inscription "I'm a Little Possum Trotter." I gave half of them away and sold the rest for one dollar.

So with my own money, I'd paid for newspaper advertisements, colored postcards, brochures, T-shirts, lapel buttons and pencils on which were written such legends as "The Prince of Pigskin Pageantry now at the Pinnacle of his Power." And "One of the Most Mysterious, Awesome Living Beings of all Times." I sent out news releases reporting incredible accomplishments of "Sudden Death" Sabol on the football field with sidebars describing his colorful campus life. And as testament to my ability, the sports editors swallowed all this stuff hook, line and sinker.

Now, football practice itself was tedious. It was a period of intense boredom punctuated by moments of acute fear. So I began writing the game program itself. And I did a column for the school newspaper entitled, "Here's a Lot from Possum Trot." I also was the team cheerleader, and I began plastering the walls of the locker room with posters and slogans and slipping fight songs onto the record player. Then I shipped off a press release to our rival, Concordia College, team's hometown paper. They were unbeaten at the time. The quote says, "Sudden Death says Colorado College will Crush Concordia College." Their game plan was simple. They wanted to break my neck. But I loved it. It makes the game more personal. This one big end was particularly anxious to break something. He seemed very capable of it, too. So at halftime I go up to the referee. I'm putting on my "choir boy look" and say, "Mr. Referee, Sir, that end—well, I hate to say it, but he's playing sorta dirty and I wish you'd watch him."

So on the first play, I asked the quarterback to call my number on an end sweep. Sure enough, this big oaf really clobbers me. I whisper in his ear, "You're nothing but chicken s---." Naturally he takes a swing and there's the referee standing right there, throwing down his flag, and yelling, "You're out of the game." We beat Concordia thirteen-to-nothing.

I had a good year. I was good enough for first-team All-Conference and we won four games, which is about twice what we normally won. The news was going all over the country about Steve "Sudden Death" Sabol. It was carried on the AP wires, and I got a letter from a disk jockey from, of all places, Possum Trot. There really is such a place, but it's in Tennessee, not Mississippi. That was fine by me because I always had a sneaking hunch I wanted to come from Tennessee anyway.

So I go back for my senior year, but I fought hepatitis all summer so I had to drop out and go back to Philadelphia and started lifting weights to get back in shape. Back in those days, most athletes didn't lift weights. Darned if I didn't work so hard at it, I was actu-ally named Mr. Philadelphia. Well I couldn't let that honor pass me by, so I had eight-by-ten photographs made showing me all aripple and holding a spear. Underneath the picture was my name and these modest words: "Acclaimed as the Greatest New Adventure Hero of the Year." That was an inspiration I got from my huge comic book collection where I have all-time favorites such as Captain America and Batman. The pictures were immediately dispatched to editors, press agents, and fans. I had the mailing addresses of influential people well catalogued from my dad's business.

That was a good start on the year but I was worried the people back in Colorado had forgotten all about me. So I went to a printer, and I had stationery made with "Universal International" and wrote all these letters. "You have been placed on Steve Sabol's mailing list and thus will be able to follow his movie career." Then came the information that Steve Sabol had been cast as a supporting actor in Universal's forthcoming film "Black Horse Troup," which is a name I got from a march by John Philip Sousa. The movie would star William Holden, Steve McQueen, Eva Marie Saint, and Steve Sabol. The letter was stamped "Approved for immedi-ate release by order of Central Casting." I'd had a stamp made up with that title on it. But I didn't send the letter to the newsmen back in Colorado Springs. They were starting to get a little suspi-cious. So instead I sent them to friends in the Colorado Springs area who were most likely to leak the news in the right places. It worked. Local columnists fell all over themselves informing the readers that "Sudden Death" Sabol was Hollywood's newest star. I must have had a hundred calls from people wanting to know if it's true that Steve McQueen is really a jerk. But I told them, "No, he's really a great guy."

So the next summer before returning for my final year of Colo-rado College, I did a grand tour of Europe and in Madrid I got inspired again. El Cordobes was the biggest bullfighter in the world at that time. There were picture postcards of him all over Spain. I said, "Now that's class." So when I got back home I shelled out some more money, actually my dad's money. I got a couple of crates of colored postcards of myself in a football uniform. On the back of the postcard is "Steve 'Sudden Death' Sabol, all-time All-Rocky Mountain Football Great." At the bottom it says "The Prince of Pigskin Pageantry." So in the fall, I go back to Colorado College. I had a new maroon convertible; I had a five-bedroom apartment even though I lived alone, but I could think better when I'm alone. I had a picture of me signing with the Cleveland Browns for $375,000. But the topper was when Coach Carle got upset because outside Washburn Stadium I put a sign that said, "Washburn Stadium, Altitude 7,989 feet," which was exactly 2,089 feet higher than it actually was but I wanted to psych-out opposing players when they came there. So I had a plaque remade for the visiting team's dressing room that read "This Field is named in Honor of Morris Washburn who perished when his lungs exploded from a lack of oxygen during a **SOCCER*** match with the University of Denver in 1901."

The Fearless Tot from Possum Trot might be the only football player in history with a better "rags to riches" story than Harry Kalas.

*More U.S. kids today play **SOCCER** than any other organized sport, including youth baseball. Perhaps, the reason so many kids play soccer is so they don't have to watch it.

So Say You One, So Say You All

Like so many kids of my generation, I grew up imitating the voice of Harry Kalas. He was my inspiration; I didn't just want to be an announcer, and I didn't just want to be a Phillies announcer. I wanted to be Harry Kalas. During those childhood and teenage years, I had no real understanding of how high I had set my sights.

As an adult, I was lucky enough to become friends with Harry through my dealings in the media, comedy and the sports banquet circuit. I will be eternally grateful to Harry, for he was the centerpiece of my comedy act.

One night, I received a call a few hours before a show, and at first I thought it was someone imitating Harry's voice because it's one of the most popular imitations in the city. Everyone has a Harry imitation. But the longer I listened, the more I realized it was actually Harry on the phone.

> I grew up imitating the voice of Harry Kalas.

"Joe, Kane and I wanted to see tonight's show, but they told me it's sold out," He said it that voice.

"Harry, no show is ever sold out for you," I quickly replied.

I'd start every show I did in Philly with a Kalas impression because Harry was money in the bank. The voice is instantly recognizable, the impression was close enough to give the audience a feeling of comfort and familiarity, and it gave me immediate credibility as an entertainer.

Truthfully, there's no other voice I enjoy doing more than his. For me, doing Harry's voice is like slipping into my favorite pair of sweat pants or sliding into the most comfortable chair in the house. Harry was always accepting of my comedy bits. Beyond that, he was congenial and encouraging. He was always a class act, even when the impression was not.

Harry would occasionally come out to see me at a comedy show, and one of the thrills of my career was the night he jumped on stage with me at the Knights of Columbus in Springfield, Delaware County. I claimed Harry's voice was so good that he could read the phone book and make it sound exciting. With that, Harry grabbed the *White Pages* and recited verbatim, "Bam-bur-ger, Har-old, P., 519 Maple Avenue, Glenolden Pennsylvania." It was orchestral.

Harry was truly a once-in-a-lifetime person. This loss is jarring, but it's also an opportunity for all of us . . . to be a little more like Harry. We imitated the voice, but a much greater calling is to emulate the man. We miss you already, H.

—**Joe Conklin**, 610 WIP

When Harry was hired in 1971, people forget how controversial it was. Bill Campbell, By Saam and Richie Ashburn were the broadcasters. Everyone had grown up on Bill Campbell. But Bill Giles had just come in to run the business side, the promotional side. He knew Harry from Houston, and he wanted him. The odd man out was Bill Campbell. Harry came into a very explosive situation. It was not a calm sea he arrived on, simply because of the love for Bill Campbell.

I was always impressed with how kind and gracious Harry was to Bill. He never slighted Bill. Bill had paid his dues. He had done the Eagles, the Warriors. Then he got the job of his dreams and he lost it, and not because he was incompetent. That said something about Harry's grace and good heart. He won the city over pretty quickly, and he was always gracious to Bill.

There really was a humbleness to his nature. He was a shy guy. He was not a boisterous hale fellow-well-met in meeting the public. He was obviously a public performer, but there was a private side to him as well—almost a shyness, in some ways. But always kind and attentive to other people.

I catch every winter in the Phillies' fantasy camp over in Clearwater—have for probably about 15 years now. And there are a number of these guys, the doctors and the dentists and the schoolteachers, they save up and they spend their $5,000 to come down for a week and be a ballplayer for four days, and hang with all the former big leaguers. They play that last day against the major league players, and for many years, Harry Kalas taped the P.A. introductions before they went to the plate. So you would hear, "No. 27, Josh Jenkins, from Villanova, PA. Jenkins." Or something like that.

I'd be back there, squatting and catching, and the campers would hear that voice. They'd step out of the batter's box, do a double-take. I'd make a comment like, "Never thought you'd hear Harry Kalas introducing you, did you?" That was always one of the highlights for those dream weekers.

—**Pat Williams**, 69, is senior vice president
for the NBA's Orlando Magic

Today I live in Mission Viejo, CA, but growing up in Kulpmont, PA, I followed the Phillies for many years through the eyes and ears of Harry Kalas. I always remembered him mentioning loyal fans on roadtrips throughout the country.

It was the summer of 1991 and the Phillies were visiting Los Angeles for a midweek series at Dodger Stadium. A coworker offered some tickets, so I decided to take my new bride to a week-night game. I knew that my grandmother, who turned 92 years old in May and is still an avid fan, would be watching the game, and we had some really big news to announce to the family: My wife was pregnant with our first child. It would be my parents' first grandchild and my grandmother's first great-grandchild. I thought, who better to announce this news to my family back in Pennsylvania than Harry Kalas during the Phillies broadcast?

I typed a brief note requesting the announcement and put it in an envelope addressed to Mr. Kalas. When I arrived at Dodger Stadium I went to the press box area and handed the envelope to a security guard with a few dollars, requesting delivery to the

Phillies broadcast booth. Without any confirmation I just knew that Harry would make the announcement.

I called my parents back in Kulpmont and told them to put a cassette in the VCR, watch and record the game. Sure enough, Harry delivered the news and delivered the script I requested by announcing that we were expecting the family's new addition. In particular, he acknowledged my grandmother, Mrs. Helen Wojcik from Kulpmont, PA, and that her grandson and his new bride were in attendance and expecting their first child. Recognizing the time-zone difference, it was very late in the evening. My grandmother told me she nearly fell out of her chair and was rendered wide awake when she heard the surprising news.

My parents still have the video recording of the game and the announcement that night, and it is a treasured memory for the Pecaitis family back in Kulpmont.

—**Frank Pecaitis**, 45, VP of GE Healthcare IT

My childhood ended the day Richie Ashburn died. It was early September 1997, and I had just moved to California for my first job after college. I already missed Philadelphia, and the news left me feeling terribly alone. Ashburn was a vital voice on the soundtrack of my youth. Now I was 22, my youth was gone, and so was Whitey.

I followed the coverage of the funeral and read Harry Kalas' poem about his friend. I wrote him a letter and Harry wrote back, enclosing a copy of the poem. That was Harry, always there when you needed him.

Until April 13, of course, when Harry died. Like Ashburn, he was on the road at the time, covering the Phillies, reliable as ever. And a city that worshipped him grieved again.

I was lucky to know Harry a little, from my years around the Vet in the early 1990s, when I published a baseball magazine from my home in Gwynedd Valley. Harry always had patience for my questions, like the time I asked for his favorite names to pronounce.

"Say-SEE-leo GWAN-tay," he began, relishing a chance to sound out the mellifluous name of a 1980s Pittsburgh reliever.

The others were Mickey Morandini, Don Carman and Alejandro Pena.

I'll miss Harry, but I have a few tapes of his old WCAU radio broadcasts with Ashburn, Andy Musser and Chris Wheeler. And because I watch baseball for a living, as a reporter for *The New York Times*, his expressions pop into my head every day.

Any well-hit ball that skips down the line, too fast for an outfielder to cut it off, is "goin' all the way to the corner!" A line drive that suddenly picks up speed and clears the fence is "goin' right on outta here . . ." That was a much different call than the no-doubter that was simply, "Outta here."

When a team reaches 11 runs in a game, to me it's always "E-oh-leven." And when somebody asks a trivia question, I always answer by saying, "How about THAT . . ." before the name. I'm aware there's no need to use the word "that" right there. But Harry did, and it sounded so perfect.

Just like everything else he ever said.

—**Tyler Kepner** covers the Yankees for *The New York Times*. When he was 13 years old, he was publishing his own baseball magazine out of his home in Gwynedd Valley, and interviewed Kalas many times.

The first time I heard that Mickey Vernon story was many years ago, and how ironic it was that they became friends later in life, living in the same area . . . When we went to Phillies games, we always stopped by the broadcast booth, and Dad was delighted that Harry was interested in what he was doing. We would see Harry in Media, at a lunch place. They were involved in the same banquets. Harry was the MC the day Marcus Hook dedicated a statue to my dad in September of '03. He sang "Take Me Out to the Ball Game." Dad was a shy, humble guy, but he was tickled.

Dad used to laugh and say he didn't remember the incident when he brought Harry into the dugout. Back then, it wasn't unusual for a thing like that to happen. Today it would be absolutely impossible to reach out and take a kid into the dugout for a half-hour . . . After Dad died, that popped up everywhere. You'd see Harry telling that story on somebody's interview program.

—**Gay Vernon**, Boston, native of Marcus Hook, PA, on the legend of her dad—a two-time AL batting champion—taking a 10-year-old Harry Kalas into the dugout at Chicago's Comiskey Park

I'm 34 years old. As a native of Lancaster, I never thought I would be working with Harry Kalas one day. When I started working for Westwood doing games, it was pretty neat to be able to tell my dad and my family and my friends back home that I was a colleague of Harry Kalas.

The crazy thing is that I did some play-by-play in college at Shippensburg. I had to tell myself to *not* sound like Harry Kalas. Of course, my voice was nothing like his, but I'd be doing baseball, I'd start into some Harry-type calls and had to tell myself to knock it off. I'm sure it's the same thing for people in New York and Marv Albert. They all tend to sound like him.

> **I had to tell myself to *not* sound like Harry Kalas.**

I've seen a lot of guys in this business just shake someone's hand and walk away and ignore the other person. Every time, Harry would stop and say something.

—**Mike Eaby**, 34, Metrolinks, Charlotte, NC

To me . . . he was my friend from Wawa, filling up his 24-oz. cup and talkin' Phillies baseball. He was a treasure, and I'll miss him.

It's funny, but that's what I remember most. At our Wawa he wasn't the Hall of Fame broadcaster. He was just Harry. He was low-key and we'd run into each other every so often and it was always special to me. Every time was the same. We'd be over by the creamers and the sugars and the Sweet n' Lows and it was as if everyone knew each other. He knew everyone's name and he wasn't a celebrity; he was just everyone's friend. He was so approachable, he was just Harry, and the talk was about how everyone was doing, and of course the Phillies.

I'm on the Board of Governors for the ALS Chapter of Greater Philadelphia and we had a special night within which we were at "Tuesdays with Morrie." Before it starts, Harry calls his son Kane on stage. Now Kane has a fabulous voice and Harry has him sing opera. Nobody blinked an eye and Kane brought down the house. Who could have pulled that off besides Harry Kalas?

Harry was special because he was the voice of our summers. He's as much a sound of summer as seagulls, barbequing hamburgers, the pop of a beer bottle cap. No matter what you are doing, you had the television on in the background during the summer just to hear that voice. I know when I'm not in the studio I watch the games at home, or I'm reading a magazine, or playing on the computer, but the game was always on and the voice was always Harry's.

Harry also understood that less is more. During those broadcasts you could hear the vendors in the background and fans calling out to him. You could hear them because he valued the silence as much as the game. He understood that baseball is a game of pauses that you didn't need to talk through. The sounds of the game came from the stands as well as the field and Harry embraced that better than anyone.

It's impossible to explain how important Harry and the next few months are going to be tough on all of us.

—**Michael Barkann**, host of CSN Sport programs

I played defensive end on the high school football team. He was a linebacker. Neither one of us played too often. Neither one of us was that good. Harry liked to play basketball, too. He could play, but not that well. He was just like a normal kid—say it that way.

I'd see him two or three times a year. He'd come out and stay with me when in Chicago on one assignment or another. He was with me at our class reunion last October. We had our 54th reunion. The ones who knew him pretty well could see he was having physical problems.

There was no one he wouldn't befriend or talk to. It could have been a bum off the street. I remember I was down in Clearwater, and we were out to dinner with our wives. There was a guy sitting at a table by himself. Harry got up and invited him to sit with us. That's the way Harry was. He was a great guy. I miss him greatly.

—**Wally Baumgartner**, 72, Aurora, IL, high school friend

I don't recall the entire story about meeting Harry, but I do remember that he came to me in Hawaii and asked the best way to go about getting a start in the broadcasting business. As I recall, 100 years ago I mentioned to him, "Harry, get together a good résumé and I'd suggest to do a ballgame live. Don't make it up because that doesn't sell real well. Ask a team for a private area where you can do a ballgame all by yourself in a recorder. If it sounds good to you, or reasonably good, send it in. But you want to give yourself the best shot at it." He ended up using a tape of an Iowa-Minnesota football game.

When Harry Kalas came to me, he was a very nice, young man. Like all guys starting out, he was very eager, which is wonderful. I told him to show enthusiasm for the game, and learn about the major-league team, even though you're going to do their affiliate's games. Learn about their major-league structure and their history, so you're not just some guy off the street who made a recording. He got started the next year and the next thing I knew, he was in the major leagues. Then, 100 years later, he was in the Hall of Fame!

But I hate thinking about that in terms of how I helped get his career going. He came to me; that's all. I didn't go seeking him out, and saying to everyone, "Hey, here's a guy I found who's going to be great." No, he came to me and I just told him what I thought. I had not heard his work, so I couldn't go up to the owners I knew or the general managers I knew and say, "Here's a young man you're going to like," because I hadn't heard his work. I just stressed to him the presentation that he could make to a team and how I would go about it. From then on out, you need talent. Harry certainly had that.

After that first meeting, we really didn't see each other or stay in touch. I was not looking for any credit along the line. I was just happy that he made it.
—**Buddy Blattner**, 90, Harry Kalas' favorite announcer,
Lake of the Ozarks, MO

There are really two great stories I love to tell. One on the television show and one here in the studio. On the television show this one time, we came to the last break and he leans over to me and whispers, "I want to sing something." I'm thinking, wow, he's not kidding me. I'm coming out of this break and I'm going to set up a song. He says "I want to sing but I don't want it to look like I asked you to sing. But I do 'High Hopes.'" So we come out of the break and I say, "Harry, I don't want to put you on the spot, but could you do a rendition of that hit song 'High Hopes.'" He lights up like a Christmas tree and by this point, he's a bad singer. I know he had been good but by this era he was not good. What I noticed was, he was way off-key but the crowd was so into it they began to sing along with him and it sounded great. We actually played it a couple of weeks ago. When they joined him, they drowned out the off-key notes and by the end they gave him a standing ovation. I said to myself, "he pulled off that rendition of 'High Hopes.' How did these people even know the words to this song?'" But they knew the words and they loved singing with Harry.

We had Harry in studio because we were celebrating the great broadcasters of Philadelphia. This was two or three years ago. He came in and I started telling him how much the fans had meant to him. The year before there had been a controversy that the Phillies had begun to push him out. I mentioned that and when that happened the call-in line exploded and everyone said if that happened they would never listen or watch another game. He started to mist up and I realized Harry didn't realize how important he was to this city. He had no ego. All he kept saying was "I'm a guy that loves his job, loves the Phillies and loves the fans of this city." I told him whether he knew it or not, they love you back like no other figure. I finished it by saying, "Harry,

I've been doing this a long time. I can tell you that the number one sports figure of the last 25 years is Harry Kalas." He shook his head no and started to rattle off great players like Michael Jack and so on. I interrupted and said, "but they all came and went and you're still here." He never believed it. He was just a guy doing his job. He was this icon and never had an ego about it. I miss him so much. It's tough to watch the game knowing he won't do a few innings. There are very few people in this world who are irreplaceable and he was one of them.

—**Angelo Cataldi**, 610 WIP Morning Show

I was working for the AP in Chicago and I met him at Wrigley. It was the first game I covered and it's the Phillies. I'm 22 and I go up to him and I said "Mr. Kalas" and I'm stammering "I'm from Philadelphia and I love you." Right away, "Anthony, come here." he puts his arm around me and brings me to the booth. I had a friend with me who was my best friend Vinny and he was living out there at the time. He invites us both in the booth and he gives us the shout out on the air "Oh, best wishes to Anthony Gargano who is now working out here in Chicago." I had called on the press box phone home to my father and my mom to listen. They loved it and thought it was great. He was so warm, we could have stayed there the whole night. After that day whenever I saw him in Chicago or New York he'd seek me out and see how I was doing. He acted like he cared and the beauty of Harry was, for that five minutes, he did care. That's all you want out of another person. That he was listening. How many people do we meet each day that ask how we are doing in a cursory fashion and don't pay attention when you start to talk to them. That's the difference. For that five minutes not only did he act like he cared, but he actually did care.

> I said "Mr. Kalas" and I'm stammering "I'm from Philadelphia and I love you."

He was the only broadcaster I ever heard. He was the guy who we all imitated in backyard Wiffle Ball or halfball and you did the lineup "Leading off for the Phillies." And of course, Michael Jack Schmidt. As great a player as Mike Schmidt was, there was a bigness that Harry gave him. Also, Mike was not the most warm and fuzzy character and Harry turned him into that. Harry was our conduit. He brought us from Lefty to Schmidt to Glenn Wilson and beyond. He was the guy that was the conduit. After that, after the Wheeze Kids died in 1983, and the Phillies were bad—for ten years they were bad—we were sports fans and Harry made it palatable.

—**Anthony L. Gargano**, 610 WIP midday, author of
The Great Philadelphia Fan Book and *A Sunday Pilgrimage*

The cool thing about Harry was he was the only broadcaster I knew growing up. His voice was just always there. I had a great-aunt Ree. She and I had virtually nothing in common. She liked my sister a whole lot more than me. But in the summer, she'd come up from Florida to live with us because it was too hot down there. She stayed in my room. She was an insanely, insanely nuts baseball fan. Every night when we went to sleep we had the baseball game on. My bedtime story was told by Harry and Whitey. Some kids got bedtime stories. I got Chico Ruiz horror stories. That's how I became a baseball fan. It was all tied in with my aunt, who I had zero in common with. We had 60 years of age difference, but we had that in common—we had Harry in common. It was the one thing we could talk about. To me there wasn't music. I've only listened to sports on the radio my whole life.

When I was 22, I got into this business and I was at a game at Veterans Stadium. At the time, I was still a smoker and there was this one spot off the press box where we were allowed to smoke. You know, with the wood paneling and the cinderblocks painted red. The thing is, everyone could smell the smoke but we were out of view so maybe that made it better. There were so many other things that could kill you at the Vet. But I'm back there by myself and I didn't remember if it was before or after the game but all of a sudden he walks around the corner. I had never met him and he didn't know who I was then and he says hello and we chit-chatted. I was so blown away I never introduced myself.

I remember getting home and calling my mom and saying "I just smoked a cigarette with Harry Kalas." Not the warm and fuzzy story you want to share with your mom, but it was Harry Kalas and that was really cool.

—**Rhea Hughes**, 610 WIP Morning Show

My summer coach, Rich Merchant is really good friends with Mike Scioscia, the manager of the Los Angeles Angels. He wanted a couple of guys to come out and help with the game, and we would get to meet Mr. Scioscia. What I did not know is that Harry Kalas was going to be there. Coach asked me if I would do my imitation of Harry Kalas. I was a little hesitant at first, even without knowing Kalas was going to be there. About the third inning of that game, I was introduced to Harry Kalas. Coach said, "This kid does a pretty good impression of you." Harry Kalas laughed and said, "All right, I'm excited to hear it." Following that, I walked up to the press box and did a Chase Utley call. It was a 2-1 pitch to Utley. It's a long drive. And his famous quote, "Chase, you are the man." After that, I walked out of the press box, and everybody in the stands was standing cheering wildly. Harry Kalas was the first person to come up to me and shake my hand. He was a great sport about it. He told me I did a great job. It was a really humbling experience for me.

All my friends were amazed about my experience. They were excited for me. It was like, "Wow. You're a celebrity."

—**Evan Cline**, senior baseball player at Strath Haven High School

While I was at Notre Dame in the early '80s, Harry had succeeded Lindsey Nelson in the "Voice of Notre Dame Highlights." I saw Harry in South Bend twice—once at a tailgating party and once at the South Bend Marriott. Both times, what stood out is that he was proudly displaying his 1980 World Series ring to those who were with him. The look of pride on his face said it all.

My second connection to Harry was in 1997, when, having moved to Boca Raton in the late '80s, I became a Marlins season ticket holder. Still, every time when the Phillies came to town, I made a point at the 7th inning to turn and salute Harry and Richie in the booth. A salute to remind myself that no matter where you are, home is just a short distance away, or in this instance, one section up behind my seats.

During the 1997 season, my wife was pregnant and when the Phils came to town that summer, I left a message at the Phillies' team hotel asking Harry if he could leave us an answering machine message to announce the eventual birth. I never expected anything to come from this except, well, perhaps the stalking police. When I got home from work, to my utter shock and surprise, my answering machine contained a message from Harry announcing that my wife and I wished for all to know that . . . "THAT BABY'S OUTTA THERE!!!" When our daughter was born in November, an inordinate number of calls were made from Vineland, New Jersey, and Ocean City, New Jersey, to our house . . . not to congratulate us, but rather to hear Harry's message to us.

There are lots of things to miss about home, like Tastykakes, cheese steaks and authentic pretzels. Sure, you can sort of get those here, or even guilt family into bringing those when they visit, but one thing that is missing and can never be replicated or reproduced in any way, shape or form, is a ballgame called by Harry Kalas. Sadly, none of us will ever experience that again.

Godspeed, Mr. Kalas.

—**George Karibjanian**, Boca Raton, Florida

 When we worked together doing Big 5 basketball, he was great, and I wasn't very good—and I learned a lot. We got to be fairly close, and Harry used to come out and play tennis with us at the Doylestown Racquet Club. We'd play four, five, six sets and then we'd go eat. Harry liked to have fun; he'd leave and beat us to the restaurant and by the time we got there he'd have had a couple

Wallbangers. We'd sit around the table and have a lot of fun. I always accused him of ordering wine by the price, rather than by the label.

He had no ego. He was just a nice guy, and he had no ego. We had a lot of fun. Harry was a fun guy to be with.

—**Bill White**, Ex-NL president and Phil Rizzuto's Yankee broadcast partner for 18 years

Even though I never knew Harry Kalas, I have a Harry story. I have the impression that almost everyone does. When I was a public relations intern with the Philadelphia Eagles in the mid 1990s, I sometimes got to do stats for visiting or third party radio crews. One of the games I had the privilege of doing was a Westwood One broadcast that featured Harry Kalas as play-by-play and **LOU HOLTZ*** as the analyst. It was tight quarters in the Vet booths and, as a South Jersey native and Phillies season-ticket holder as a kid, I was ecstatic to sit shotgun with the voice that had provided so much background to my childhood. This same voice determined one of my all-time favorite Phils to be little known '80s middle reliever Porfi Altamirano, not because of his pitching exploits, but due to his radio introduction.

In the game day program for the contest, I had written an article on Jermane Mayberry and the Eagles' Eye Mobile he sponsored. Prior to kickoff in the booth, everyone was busy with their pre-game prep and responsibilities. I seized the moment during a break and asked Mr. Kalas if he could please sign my article if it was not too much trouble. "You wrote this article?" he asked. After confirming that I did, he proceeded to read it. I was somewhat shocked, considering time was winding down before kickoff and this was THE Harry Kalas. I remember feeling as though I was going to get in trouble for taking up his time. After he was done he told me it was a very good article, and that I should be proud of it. I was. He then slid the program to Coach

*When **LOU HOLTZ** was coaching Arkansas, his personal attorney was Bill Clinton.

Holtz, who was understandably busy with his pregame prep. Also a very nice man. Mr. Holtz began to sign the program before being halted by Mr. Kalas. "No Lou," he said. "You need to sign on this page. Kevin wrote the article." Lou complied and I was given back what is now my most cherished piece of memorabilia—an Eagles game day program with a Harry Kalas autograph and 1½ Lou Holtz autographs.

—**Kevin Lorincz**, sports information director, Rutgers

Philly baseball, for me, has always been Harry Kalas. I'm into tattoos. I had already scheduled an appointment when Harry passed. When I got there, Rob Fiore, my artist in Montgomeryville, Pennsylvania, and I were talking and I said I would be very interested in having a "Harry" tattoo, eventually. He said, "Man, let's just do it today."

We went on Google for a couple of hours and searched through the pictures looking for the one to be able to capture him the best and where he could get all the detail for the tattoo and not be guessing. I wanted to be sure we would be able to recognize who it was. It took four hours for him to do it, and he charged me $300. He usually charges $100 an hour.

The newspaper called and asked if they could come over and photograph it. When the photographer saw it, he said, "Dude, I want to throw this on You-Tube, not just the website." He placed it on YouTube, and it's been crazy ever since. You just type in "Harry Kalas Tattoo" and the video will come up.

I've been getting tattoos for a while now, and my parents disapprove of most of them. But, this one—my dad was going nuts. He loved it, and he was all excited. He called and told all his friends. He was proud of me, I guess!

—**Mike Schwarz**, 22, Phillie fanatic

My husband, Alan, had ALS. In 1983, there was an article that appeared in the *Philadelphia Inquirer* about me and my husband, and in it our family talked about ALS. Nancy Giles saw it. My mother, who passed away in January, got an introduction to Nancy Giles and told her baseball ought to get involved with ALS, that this belonged in baseball. And that's how we became the charity of the Phillies' wives.

But before there was an event, or anything like that, the next year the Phillies arranged for my family to come to a game and have a booth at the Vet. My husband was seriously ill at that time; he could not walk. Really barely could sit up. But he was a rabid fan. We got to the booth, and at the Vet you had to walk down these steps if you wanted to sit where you could look out at the field. So our aide literally picked up my husband and carried him down to his seat. We were all sitting there, and we looked up . . . and Harry was in the booth next door, sobbing. He didn't know us, had never met us, but he watched this whole thing happen.

My mother, who was a character, saw him and went over to him and said, "Did you know this is what Lou Gehrig went through?" Harry said, "Whatever you need from me, I'll be there for you." And for the next 25 years, Harry worked at every event, he MC'd every fashion show we did, he did every autograph party, which is now the Phillies Phestival. Every year he was the MC of our annual luncheon. Well, every year but one—and that was the year we honored him.

Lots of people say that: "Anything you want, I'll do." But he did. He kept us promise for 25 years.

This last year, I saw him in December at our annual luncheon. Harry was such a master of his craft. I actually said it to the audience that day: Harry takes nothing for granted. I fax him what's happening, he brings his notes, we sit down and go over everybody's pronunciation. He makes sure he has everything right. It's like the old joke—how do you get to Carnegie Hall? Practice, practice, practice. Well, how do you get to be a Hall of

Fame broadcaster? Practice, practice, practice. He was such a pro, and always in the background. He was never there for the limelight. He was there for the ALS cause, and to keep that cause in front of people as much as possible.

There was no ego to him. It's unusual to find somebody as nice, and humble, and as grounded as he was.

He loved our families, and he knew them by name. He would see me at the ballpark and ask about our patients by name. He'd say, "How's Shelby?" I always got holiday cards from him. He brought Kane to an event we did in Delaware, around Christmastime, and he and Kane sang "White Christmas," and ended with "High Hopes." He made everybody smile.

At the Phillies Phestival, we bring in the families a little early so they can meet the players prior to the crush and spend a little time with them. Harry was always there, he was always on the field meeting the sponsors. He made so many people happy, by being there and doing all these things.

Harry's wife Eileen had an uncle who had ALS. Two years ago, Harry donated a lot of his library to the ALS Association—all the books that he had gotten, and personalized. Some of them, he signed them. A lot of them, the author who had given them to Harry had signed them. He asked us to use them, and we auctioned some, gave them as gifts to patients, gifts to sponsors. It was so generous of him.

He could be eating dinner, in the middle of a bite of food, and I'd say, "Harry, can you come and meet this patient?" Down would go the food, and off he'd go. He's a mensch; what can I say? That's my favorite word to describe Harry. He was extraordinary.

—**Ellyn Phillips**, President, Great Philadelphia ALS Association

WE WON'T BE RIGHT BACK AFTER THIS

Kent Tekulve

Kent Tekulve was known for his unique submarine delivery, and was one of the best and most durable relievers in baseball during a 16-year career. Tekulve became a broadcaster after he retired, working for the Phillies before becoming an analyst for FSN in Pittsburgh. He held the chair next to Harry Kalas the night after Richie Ashburn passed away.

Richie Ashburn was responsible for my best and my worst days as a broadcaster. I got to sit in for Whitey the day he got inducted into the Hall of Fame. Scott Graham and I did the radio; Harry was off in Cooperstown with his buddy Whitey while Whitey was getting inducted. I got to sit in the analyst chair that day in Wrigley Field, and the cool part for me was, I had the Richie Ashburn pregame show. The previous Wednesday, before Whitey took off for Cooperstown, we sat down and did the pregame show—and I interviewed him about going into the Hall of Fame. So not only did I get to sit in Whitey's chair, I did the Richie Ashburn Show with Whitey, talking about the Hall of Fame. It was the highlight of my career.

> Richie Ashburn was responsible for my best and my worst days as a broadcaster.

My worst day was when Whitey passed away. I was flying in the day before to do the day game against the Mets. When I arrived at the hotel, I find out that Whitey has passed away. I hadn't heard about it on the way over. Because Andy Musser and Chris Wheeler were doing TV that night, it basically came down to this: I was the only person in town to help Harry out on radio that night.

They called me after I get to the hotel and said, "We need you to work with Harry." Well, first of all, I'm not a radio broadcaster. I've only done a handful of games on radio in my life. But you do what you've got to do. We go to the ballpark, and Harry is devastated. Just devastated. He's lost his best friend. This morning has been one of the worst days of his life. I make a decision that I'm just going to stay out of the way as best I can, and just be there to do whatever I can do to help Harry get through this—including if we get to a certain point in the game where he can't go on or he chokes up, I'm going to have to jump in and do play-by-play, which I've never done in my life, but we're going to get through this thing.

This is not an opportunity for me; I'm there for Harry. This is something we've just got to get through. We go to the ballpark, there's not much conversation, and I'm in panic mode. Harry is devastated. There's very little conversation at dinner; some talk about Whitey, but everybody knows what Harry is going through, so nobody is sure whether they ought to get into that in front of him because nobody knew what it would do to Harry.

Finally we go to the radio booth. It's getting close to time to go on. I look over, and his scorecard only has names on it. That's it. His scorecard is usually full of notes and information he'll use during the game. But this night, just two lineups. His head is down, his chin is on his chest. And I'm thinking: This is going to be a really rough night for him.

Then the cue comes that it's time to start the show. He's sitting there with his head down, expressionless, names only on his scorecard, and the guy tells him: "Go." And suddenly he starts: "Good evening, everyone, welcome to Shea Stadium . . ." and he's flowing like he always does. We talk about the game, we go through the introduction, we talk about Whitey, he goes through the whole thing. We make it through the first inning—and I'm watching him, just marveling that this sounds exactly like Harry.

Unfortunately for all the folks at home, this is radio. They can't see what I see, which is this man—who is devastated—doing his job, just barely marking his scorecard with flyout to left field and no semblance of what he normally does. He says, "At the end of the first inning, the Mets and Phillies are scoreless." And as soon as we go to break—boom—his head drops down, just like before we started. We go through the entire game, and this goes on all night long. But this broadcast, in obviously the worst situation he's ever going to be in, sounds as much like it can as every other broadcast he's ever done to the people at home—other than, obviously, the emotion that came up when we talked about Whitey.

I would venture to say, over the course of the entire evening, if I said 50 words, I said a lot. I just sat there the entire night and watched him. I was there to be the safety net. And this man put on a performance that was as professional as anything I've ever seen in my life—including some pretty darn good baseball players putting on some pretty good performances. But this man being able to do his job no matter what the circumstances—and these were obviously the worst possible—was just amazing to me. I just sat there with my mouth open, just watching him.

> "For Kent Tekulve, for our technicians, and everyone else . . . and for Richie Ashburn . . . I'm Harry Kalas. Good night, everybody."

And every half inning, you'd get a reminder of just how devastated he was. His head would drop right back down to his chest. There was just the two of us and a technician in the booth, no cameras, nothing. We just kept looking at each other and kind of saying: How is he doing this?

At the end of the night, the game is over, we did the wrap up, and Harry wrapped it up with, "For Kent Tekulve, for our technicians, and everyone else . . . and for Richie Ashburn . . . I'm Harry Kalas. Good night, everybody." When he included Whitey in the wrap, there's no way I could have done it. I wouldn't even have attempted it.

So now we're off the air, we're collecting our things, putting our stuff away. We stood up and just looked at each other. I walk two steps over to him and gave him a big hug, and without saying a word, we turned around and walked out of the booth. As we're walking out of the booth, I had two distinct thoughts that kept running through my head. One was that this was the most professional performance I've ever seen. I'd never seen anything like this from someone in the circumstances he was under.

The second, a polar opposite thought, was: I hope the people who were listening to this broadcast and listening to how professional it was and how well it was done understood what happened. I hope no one thought that the stuff about Harry and Whitey being such good friends must have been bunk, because he didn't sound like he was all that affected, because of the way the night had gone. I was really concerned people listening might have that reaction, that they really weren't that close and they'd been duped all these years. Because it was radio; they couldn't see what I could see. That's how professional he'd been, what a great manner he'd carried himself in through that night. No one else saw how devastated he was, when he was allowed to be devastated—when his professionalism didn't dictate that he had to be professional, how devastated he was during those two-minute breaks. Because when those breaks were over, he found a way to continue.

Because it was radio; they couldn't see what I could see.

My relationship with Harry outside of that night was like everybody else's. But that night was a doozy.

Your relationship with Harry had nothing to do with your stature. Mike Schmidt, Mickey Morandini, Ozzie Virgil, they were all the same to him: they were Phillies.

He became more involved publicly with Schmidt or with Steve Carlton because of the home run calls or the more poignant moments. But the thing with Harry was, if you were a Fightin'—as he liked to call us—you were one of his guys. He enjoyed being around you as much as you enjoyed being around him. And that stems directly from his relationship with Whitey, I think. He had a way of understanding, better than most, what it was like to have done it, what it was like to go out and compete every day, and have good days and have bad days and have these shining moments and have these down moments.

He got just as much joy out of calling a home run by Luis Aguayo—Long Ball Luis, Harry called him—as he did a home run by Gary Matthews. For Harry, it was just that one of the Fightin's was doing something good.

He was a good friend to everybody on that ballclub—and not only us, but everybody who was there, the people working around the ballpark, the fans, the ushers, the grounds crew. Everybody was the same. The governor could come into the ballpark, and the guy selling pretzels on the corner could come into the ballpark, and to Harry those were the same people. It didn't matter to him. He just enjoyed being around people who liked his Fightin's.

Harry Kalas and Richie Ashburn in pre-game interview.

TO BE CONTINUED!

We hope you have enjoyed *Remembering Harry Kalas*. Due to space and time considerations over a dozen people with wonderful stories did not make the book. However, you can look for their stories in the author's forthcoming book: *For Phillies Fans Only*. Also coming soon from the author is *For Eagles Fans Only*. You can be included in either or both books if you have an interesting story involving either the Phillies or the Eagles. Email it to printedpage@cox.net (please put PHILLLIES FANS or EAGLES FANS in the subject line and be sure to include a phone number where you can be reached), or call the author directly at (602) 738-5889.

OTHER BOOKS BY RICH WOLFE

Da Coach (Mike Ditka)
I Remember Harry Caray
There's No Expiration Date on Dreams (Tom Brady)
He Graduated Life with Honors and No Regrets (Pat Tillman)
Take This Job and Love It (Jon Gruden)
Been There, Shoulda Done That (John Daly)
Oh, What a Knight (Bob Knight)
And the Last Shall Be First (Kurt Warner)
Remembering Jack Buck
Sports Fans Who Made Headlines
Fandemonium
Remembering Dale Earnhardt
For Yankee Fans Only
For Cubs Fans Only
For Red Sox Fans Only
For Cardinals Fans Only
For Packers Fans Only
For Hawkeye Fans Only
For Browns Fans Only
For Mets Fans Only
For Notre Dame Fans Only—The New Saturday Bible
For Bronco Fans Only
For Nebraska Fans Only
For Buckeye Fans Only
For Georgia Bulldog Fans Only
For South Carolina Fans Only
For Clemson Fans Only
For Cubs Fans Only—Volume II
For Oklahoma Fans Only
For Yankee Fans Only—Volume II
I Saw It On the Radio (Vin Scully)
Tim Russert, We Heartily Knew Ye

All books are the same size, format and price.
Questions? Contact the author directly at 602-738-5889.